ANSWERS FOR PARISH COUNCILLORS

Answers

for

Parish Councillors

William J. Rademacher

With Three Chapters on the History,
the Theology, and the Future of the Parish

TWENTY-THIRD PUBLICATIONS
P.O. Box 180   Mystic, CT 06355

ISBN 0-89622-134-2
Library of Congress Catalog Card No. 81-51429

Edited by Carol McGarry
Designed by John G. van Bemmel
Cover by SAK Group

Preface

It's been over ten years since I wrote *Answers for Parish Councils*. At that time, most parish councils were just getting organized. Wrestling with the normal problems of beginners, they were trying to get a grip on their identity and purpose in a fast-changing church. They were concerned about constitutions and their advisory or decision-making status.

While some of these problems are still with us, they are no longer in the forefront. Most councils have grown toward a greater maturity and are now facing new questions. They are more concerned about ministry and mission, about goal-setting and the development of pastoral teams.

In the fall of 1979, I wrote *The Practical Guide for Parish Councils*, published by Twenty-Third Publications. It discusses a wide variety of parish council problems, including those of formation and organization. With the publication of the *Guide* and the growth of councils during the past ten years, much of the material in the original *Answers for Parish Councils* had become either obsolete or repetitious. It soon became evident that *Answers for Parish Councils* had to be revised.

In this major revision, I have eliminated some of the questions of beginners, either because they were no longer pertinent to the councils of the 80's or because they have been treated rather thoroughly in *The Practical Guide for Parish Councils.*

I have added many questions and answers (about 70% are new); I feel these speak more directly to the councils of the 80's. With minor revisions, these were first published in *Today's Parish* magazine by Twenty-Third Publications.

I have also added three entirely new chapters dealing with the history, theology, and future of the parish. I feel these chapters will be helpful to councils as they assume greater responsibilities in shaping the parish of the 80's.

As this book goes to press, I am grateful to Gonzaga University,

Spokane, Washington, for offering me The Flannery Chair of Catholic Theology during the 1979-80 academic year. Without the opportunity for writing and research provided by the Chair, this book would still be nothing more than a dream.

My thanks also to Sister Pat Boyd for her extra care in correcting, typing, and then retyping the entire manuscript.

I hope and pray that these words will minister to the continuing growth of parish councils in the church of the 80's. I hope by God's grace that I too may share in that growth in Christ Jesus. I pray that together we can "go forward on the road that has brought us to where we are" (Philippians 3:16).

William J. Rademacher
Institute for Parish Ministries
Gonzaga University
Spokane, Washington
July 1, 1980

CONTENTS

Introduction

The parish is in trouble. "The modern parish is hopelessly outdated," writes Bishop John Mussio formerly of Steubenville, Ohio. Father John Foster entitles his book *Requiem for a Parish*. In it, he offers considerable support to show that the parish in its present form "has ... had its day."[1]

Bishop Albert Ottenweller of Steubenville, Ohio, received loud and long applause from his fellow bishops in November 1975, when he called for a total restructuring of the parish. In April 1979, he analyzed the parish in greater depth. Speaking at a regional meeting in New York, he said:

> Parishes today are very weak ... they are not doing their job. One reason the parish is weak is ... that institution is very strong but community is very weak .... Our instincts are toward institution, toward programs, projects and services; they are not toward community.[2]

Fr. Philip Murnion, the executive director of the United States Catholic Bishops' parish project, lists other weaknesses of today's parish:

> One weakness of the parish is its tendency to develop ministry in terms of its existing structures, rather than to develop ministerial structures around existing needs. A second weakness is the tendency in the parish for large numbers of people to be rather anonymous and not to have the opportunity for a more personal, communal relationship in the context of which they can deepen their faith and reflect on their lives. A third weakness of the parish is that there remains a tendency for parish ministry to be highly professionalized, for the ministry to be contained within the hands of the clergy and religious. A fourth weakness of the parish is the tendency of the parish's view of life to be restricted to its borders.[3]

---

* The first three chapters are an expansion of my Flannery Lecture given at Gonzaga University, Spokane, Washington, on April 11, 1980.

While some are ready to sing a requiem for the parish, others, like Archbishop Casey of Denver, "believe the time has come to reassert the importance of the parish." In its present form, the parish has been with us for over a thousand years. No doubt, it will be with us, in one form or another, for many years to come.

However, there seems to be a growing consensus that the parish, as we know it today, needs to be re-evaluated and seriously restructured. Because of the developments of postconciliar theology and because of the sociology of a rapidly changing culture, many questions are challenging today's parish. While some of these questions are primarily cultural and sociological, others are definitely theological. A few examples will suffice.

1. In view of Vatican II's emphasis on the People of God, and in view of our highly mobile society and the complex relational patterns of modern urban living, should not the territorial principle of parish organization, consecrated by canon law, be abandoned in favor of more personal community-building principles?

2. With the emergence of lay ministers, to what "level" of the church will these ministers be held accountable? Some dioceses insist on certifying eucharistic ministers; most parishes, on the other hand, feel responsible for training ministers and installing them publicly in some kind of paraliturgical ceremony. Full-time lay ministers receive their salary from the parish, not from the diocese. For this reason, they feel accountable to the parish. What specific community will be responsible for the support, evaluation, and spiritual growth of these ministers? In other words, who is responsible for the non-ordained ministers, the parish or the diocese?

3. To what extent are parishes free to determine their own pastoral mission, with consequent allocation of ministering personnel and material resources? Can a parish, for instance, decide on its own that it will not accept a diocesan assessment for a diocesan high school because it decides the school is not part of its pastoral priority? Is it possible to move toward a more autonomous, more independent model of parish and, at the same time, avoid the dangers of congregationalism?

4. Must a parish still try to respond to the social needs of its parishioners with dances and coffee houses? Or should it concen-

trate its dwindling resources on more spiritual and apostolic activities like evangelization?

5. What should be the missionary commitment of the parish to the spiritual and material poverty of the Third World?

6. With the emergence of team ministers, whose view of the nature and mission of the parish shall prevail? To what ecclesial community do the team members relate? Does the priest relate to the diocesan church? The sister, to her religious community? The layperson, to the parish?

7. How will the new "base communities" relate to the parish?

8. Since Vatican II, the church has emphasized community as essential for the celebration of the liturgy. It has also approached the Eucharist as a fellowship meal. Is not the modern parish rather far removed both from community and from the intimacy implied in a fellowship meal?

PART ONE

The History, Theology, and Future of the Parish

CHAPTER ONE

The History of the Parish

The modern parish is the product of a long and complicated historical development. In its basic outline, it was shaped, first, by the faith of the believers who responded to God's call and, second, by the historical and cultural conditions in which these believers lived. A brief history of this development may be helpful.

"Parish" in the Bible

The word *parish* comes from the Greek verb *paroikeo* meaning "to dwell by, beside or near; to dwell as a stranger or alien without citizenship." It refers to man's temporary sojourn in this life. This verb is used sixty times in the Septuagint version of the Old Testament. It usually means "to be a stranger, to sojourn, to dwell temporarily in a foreign country."

In the Old Testament period, the noun *paroikia* (parish) means "the exile or sojourner in a strange land without citizenship or right of domicile ... as opposed to the home country."[4]

The noun *paroikos* (sojourner), which is used forty times in the Old Testament, refers to "the immigrant, the alien, the exile." Thus, Abraham is a *paroikos* or foreigner in Egypt (Genesis 17:10); Lot is a *paroikos* or foreigner in Sodom (Genesis 19:9); Isaac is a foreigner in Canaan.

While the word *paroikia* is Greek, part of its religious meaning comes out of the faith experience of the Hebrew community. God called Abraham, demanding a total uprooting from the land where he lived. He asked him to go to a foreign land to become the father of innumerable descendants. These descendants would become a community because they would be united by a threefold bond: 1) the call; 2) the promise; and 3) the covenant. Abraham and his people would always remain foreign dwellers. They would form a parish (*paroikia*), that is to say, a community of pilgrims living in a borrowed land. "To form part of this Hebrew community of foreigners, it was necessary to join the covenant through faith."[5] It was a covenant made on man's side by transients, not land-owners. Faith, not land, united the covenanted community.

The Israelites formed a real parish in Egypt. While living as slaves in the midst of a pagan people, they nevertheless remained faithful to the covenant, desiring to continue their pilgrimage to the Promised Land.[6]

The word *parish* acquired another part of its religious meaning from the Hebrew understanding of *assembly* (in Hebrew *qahal*; in Greek *ekklesia*). In the Old Testament, this assembly is the result of four distinct activities: first, the assembly is called together by the supreme authority of the people in the name of God; second, the assembly listens to the Word of God and an explanation; third, the assembly responds to the Word of God by some religious action, a sacrificial rite, a blessing, or a thanksgiving; fourth, the assembly is dismissed by the presiding official.[7]

In the New Testament, the word *parish* (or its derivatives) is rarely used. (Luke 24:18; Hebrews 11:9; Acts 7:6,29; Ephesians 2:19; 1 Peter 2:11; Acts 13:17; 1 Peter 1:17). However, when it is used, it retains its Old Testament meaning of aliens dwelling in a foreign land. In addition, it acquires a more mystical meaning. "The Christian knows that his life in the world is only of a temporary nature. His real fatherland for which he was born is heaven. He is on earth as a pilgrim."[8]

In the New Testament, the word church (*ekklesia*) and parish (*paroikia*) have, for all practical purposes, the same meaning. Since the early Christian communities are awaiting the imminent return of the Lord, they think of themselves as pilgrims without a permanent homeland here on earth; that is, they see themselves as a *paroikia* (a parish).

In the New Testament, therefore, the parish is not a community of neighbors who live around a fixed place of worship; nor is it a territorial district. Rather, it is a community of faith living as a stranger and pilgrim in this world.

The faith of the community is more important than the place where it assembles. The Jerusalem community, for instance, gathers for prayer and Word services in three different places: 1) in the temple (Acts 2:4f), indicating some continuity with Israel; 2) in one house after the other, for the breaking of the bread; and 3) on the porch of Solomon's temple (Acts 5:12).

No matter where it assembles, the New Testament community carries out a three-fold mission: 1) preaching; 2) worship; and 3) pastoral care. The apostles, of course, have an important role in the preaching mission (Acts 6:2-4). In the Pauline communities, however, *all* the members share some responsibility for proclaiming the Word. Thus, we read in 1 Corinthians 14:26: "When you come together each of you has a hymn, has an instruction, has a revelation, has a tongue, has an interpretation. Let all things be done unto edification."

Besides the celebration of the Eucharist, the community's worship consists of baptism, imposition of hands (Acts 8:17-19), and singing of psalms, hymns, and spiritual songs (Ephesians 5:19-21). Pastoral care is modeled on the image of the Good Shepherd and the service of slaves (*douloi*). The ministries of pastoral care range from the ministry of the Word to the ministry of temporal administration. The Christian community is formed by its song, by its mission, and by its celebrations.

In the New Testament, the church refers to itself both as *paroikia* (parish) and as *ekklesia* (church). When it is looking at itself in relation to this earth, as a pilgrim passing through, it refers to itself as *paroikia* (parish). When it is looking at itself in its relation to God, as fellow citizens of the saints and members of God's household, it refers to itself as *ekklesia* (church). Naturally, both words are used in a non-technical sense, more descriptive than definitive.

In early Christianity, there is no established pattern of church organization. The first Christian communities are formed in the major cities (Jerusalem, Antioch, Corinth, Ephesus). Initially, a small community of families gather together in one house for Word and prayer services. Such "house churches" could hold little more than sixty people.[9] These "house churches" continue until the first half of the third century. In the pastoral letters, Paul insists that church leaders be distinguished by their virtue of hospitality (1 Timothy 3:2; Titus 1:7-9). No doubt, they are expected to volunteer their houses as places for Christian worship.

In terms of church organization, Jean Colson distinguishes two main lines of development. The first is Paul's line, which has a college of presbyters but no bishop or president. Unity is based, not on a single leader, but on the theology of the body of Christ with many members and many distinct functions. Presbyteral communities (no bishop) survived long into post-apostolic times, especially in Alexandria, Egypt.

The second form of community organization is characterized by a single leader, a monarchic bishop, who resides in the community. This leader is the image of the living unity of the community. He is one who can be seen and touched.

After the apostolic period, this monarchical community (one bishop) emerges as the dominant form of church organization. Ignatius of Antioch (c. 107) leans heavily on this monarchic model to protect his flock from the triple threat posed by the gnostics, docetists, and judaizers. And it works. It saves his flock from "heresy." But, as is the case in Antioch, the gradual dominance of monarchic or episcopal communities is the end result of the church's response to specific historical situations; it is not the result or application of a set body of doctrine regarding church organization.

Episcopal Communities

From Ignatius of Antioch to the Council of Nicaea (325), the local church is shaped by the twofold dynamic of ministry and geography. In the cities, the bishop is, at first, the ordinary pastor of the community. He presides over the Eucharist and administers the sacraments. *Parish* priests don't exist. However, the city bishop has priests, deacons, and deaconesses around him to assist him in his pastoral and charitable work. In the second and third centuries, the city is divided into regions which are placed under a deacon or priest who remains subject to the bishop. These regions are not parishes because the city bishop is still the direct superior of the entire district.

Until the Council of Nicaea, there is no evidence that territory is a principle of church organization. In the cities the dominant model of church organization is that of a pastor-bishop surrounded by deacons and presbyters who go out from the bishop's altar to minister to the outlying districts of the city.

As the church spreads from the city into the country, presbyters are sent out into the surrounding villages. However, very soon these rural villages are cared for by *rural* bishops (*chorepiscopoi*). At first, these rural bishops are equal to the city bishops. Gradually, however, the rural bishops become subject to the city bishops. They may not ordain priests without the permission of the city bishop. Rural bishops become very numerous. In the West, especially in Africa, bishops are appointed to every hamlet and village. "In 397, Aurelius, Bishop of Carthage, had an episcopal consecration almost every Sunday."[10] In the East rural bishops are also very numerous. The canons specify "that a community must number at least twelve Christian males before a bishop could be elected."[11]

After Constantine (337), the numerous rural bishops begin to yield to the itinerant bishops who represent the city bishops. These rural bishops are poorly educated and, therefore, susceptible to heresy and schism. Gradually, rural bishops begin to fade out of the picture. Priests begin to replace the bishops in taking care of the pastoral work. Pope Leo I (440-61) forbids the installation of bishops in small villages and demands that the people be satisfied with a simple priest. From now on, priests in growing numbers become responsible for the rural villages.

Priests also become responsible for the titular churches which originally are house-churches with private, secular owners. The church gradually acquires these house-churches and equips them with baptistries. Naturally, these communities are very small. Administered by married priests, these house-churches generally remain in the priest's family through inheritance from one generation of priests to the next.

Before Nicaea, both in the East and in the West, the development of the "parish" is uneven and extremely complex. Just about every principle of the church organization has numerous exceptions. Since before Constantine, the church doesn't own property, (again there are exceptions), its methods of organization are almost infinitely flexible, constantly adapting to existing needs and structures. In general, church organization is determined more by sociological and political circumstances (the synagogue, trade routes, Graeco-Roman culture) than by theological or doctrinal considerations.

Within this incredible variety of church organization, only three principles emerge with any consistency. First, territory or property with boundaries is not the determining factor in defining the local church. Second, the rural priest always remains the delegate of the city bishop. He comes from the altar of the bishop and is responsible to him. This remains true even when priests are appointed to the regions of the city. Third, the priest does not ordain other priests. In the Western church, he does not perform the chrismation (the anointing with chrism) even when, in the absence of the bishop, he begins to administer baptism. Thus, chrismation or confirmation is gradually separated from baptism.

"Parishes" After Constantine

In 294, the emperor Diocletian divided the Roman Empire into regional districts called dioceses. After Constantine, the church adopted this Roman system and organized itself along the lines of the Roman dioceses. In this way, the territory governed by a Roman Civil magistrate is also governed by a church magistrate, such as the bishop. This is not a sudden development. In some areas, "parish" and "diocese" are used for the same district. The bishop, however, is the sole lawgiver and the administrator of all church property. The clergy remain under the bishop, pastorally, personally, and economically.

Also, after Constantine, the church begins to own property in its own name. The diocese becomes a juridical person under Roman law. Gradually, individual churches become juridical persons too, and they acquire property in their own name.

With their new freedom guaranteed by the edict of Milan (313), Christians build oratories, churches, and monasteries at a terrific rate. Often, they are built on the graves of saints, reflecting the growing cult of the dead which is especially evident in the rural communities.

1. Baptismal Churches   In the fifth century, two types of parishes develop, especially in Gaul and Spain. First in importance are the baptismal churches. These have a baptismal font, and baptism is regularly celebrated there. The second type of church, located in the smaller villages, has no baptismal font. It is dependent on the baptismal churches.

In the fifth century, the bishop begins to appoint the resident archpriests to the baptismal churches. In the sixth century, he gives the archpriest the right to baptize and preach, which formerly had been reserved to the bishop. In the ninth century, the archpriest receives the right to conduct funerals. Numerous clergy begin to gather around the baptismal churches. Often they live in community. Their wives live separately with the servants.

2. Privately Owned Churches   In the eighth century, baptismal churches are gradually replaced by privately owned churches (*eigenkirchen*). Such churches are often the property of individual laity or of families. The layman is the landlord of the church. He can sell, bequeath, or give it away. From the income, he has to maintain the priest and pay for the expenses of maintaining the church. He can keep whatever money is left. Privately owned churches are among the most advantageous capital investments of that period. In 826 two Roman Synods give papal approval to the system of privately owned churches. This system lasted from the middle of the seventh until the end of the ninth century. The custom of the priest expecting a stole fee for the administration of the sacraments (with stole) originated with the privately owned churches. In some cases, the stole fee was the priest's only means of support.

In the ninth and tenth centuries, this system declined as a result of numerous abuses which reduced the management of church property to a lucrative trade. The Gregorian Reform, which culminated in the first and second Lateran Councils (1123 and 1139), reserves to bishops alone the right to appoint priests to churches. Lay ownership of churches is now forbidden. The decrees of the Lateran Councils are so rigorously enforced that privately owned churches cease to exist by the end of the twelfth century.

3. The Benefice System   From the tenth century to the Council of Trent (1545-63), the parish is shaped by the acceptance of the benefice system, by the adoption of the tithe as a system of support, by the building of parish schools, by lay involvement in temporal administration, and by an increase in social activities centered around the parish.

The benefice system begins to evolve in the sixth century; however, it is not adopted by the universal church until the eleventh. A benefice, in its developed form, can be defined as a legal entity permanently constituted or erected by a competent ecclesiastical authority and consisting of a sacred office and the right to receive the revenue accruing from the endowment of such office. A benefice has four main characteristics: 1) perpetuity; 2) the right to revenue from church property; 3) a formal decree of ecclesiastical authority giving to certain funds or property the character or title of a benefice; 4) an annexed office of spiritual functions such as the care of souls or the exercise of jurisdiction.

What is important about a benefice is the endowment which goes with it. This consists of the goods owned by the benefice, the obligatory payments of some family, the voluntary offerings of the faithful, and the stole fees which are payable to the priest who holds the office attached to the benefice. Important, too, is the fact that a benefice has an objective perpetuity. It continues to exist even after the priest who holds it is transferred or dies. It has a legal existence all by itself. Thus, there arises a clear distinction between the benefice, the office, and the priest. Also, property or endowment becomes an important element in the chemistry of the parish.

In the context of the parish, the office is the position or chair of directing and running the parish and of performing the spiritual functions required in the care of souls. The appointment to office is gradually reserved to the bishop, who can appoint an ordained or non-ordained person. In practice, he appoints an ordained priest who then gets his room and board from the revenues of the benefice.

The adoption of the tithe as a system of church support requires members of the parish to contribute ten percent of their income in produce or grain to their parish. It has its origin in the Old Testament Mosaic Law. As early as 585, the tithe becomes obligatory, both by civil and by ecclesiastical law (under pain of excommunication). The practical effect of the tithe is to tie parishioners more closely to a particular parish. They have a right to expect sacramental services from the parish which receives their tithe. In the absence of any territorial principle, the tithe becomes the bond of belonging.

In 845 some parishes begin to build schools. "Bishop Hincmar of Rheims expresses his desire to build a school in every parish."[12]

At this time, too, the church becomes the center for social and business activities: "... purchase of gifts and all public acts took place there. Slaves were freed before the altar. The church served as archive and often enough in the country as a barn or threshing floor. It provided sanctuary for fugitives, but was also used for legal processes, banquets, plays and dancing."[13]

In thirteenth century Germany, the laity have the right to vote in selecting their own parish priest. They have presentation and nomination rights. In France, it is common practice for laypersons to be responsible for the temporal administration of the parish.

Throughout the Middle Ages, the civil and parish community are basically one and the same. Serving both ecclesial and secular interests, it is at the same time church and civil community.

The Council of Trent

The parish as we know it today was basically shaped during and after the Council of Trent. Now the parish priest becomes responsible for the care of souls. The faithful of the diocese are divided into clearly defined parishes, each served by its own parish priest. The Council deals with the problem of the parish in its twenty-fourth session:

... In those cities and localities where the parochial churches have no definite boundaries, and whose rectors have not their own people whom they may rule but administer the sacraments indiscriminately to all who desire them, the holy council commands the bishops that, for the greater security of the salvation of the souls committed to them, they divide the people into definite and distinct parishes and assign to each its own permanent parish priest, who can know his people and from whom alone they may licitly receive the sacraments; or that they make other, more beneficial provisions as the conditions of the locality require. They shall also see to it that the same is done as soon as possible in those cities and localities where there are no parish churches; any privileges and customs whatsoever, even though immemorial, notwithstanding.[14]

After Trent, the territorial principle, with clearly established boundaries, becomes the norm for establishing parishes. There are some exceptions; the *personal* principle is used to establish special parishes for those who belong to different rites and for those who belong to national minorities, such as Polish or Slovak.

Yet it is mainly the parishioners living within clearly defined boundaries who constitute the average parish. Even though, in principle, each parish is supposed to have its own church, Rome does, by way of exception, allow several parishes to use the same church.

With the Council of Trent the division and establishment of new parishes is reserved to the bishop. After him, the parish priest has exclusive authority over the parishioners. He receives the right to baptize and to anoint the sick. He is charged with the duty to preach on Sundays and during Lent and Advent. He must from now on keep a register of all baptisms and marriages.

Lay Christians now become passive subordinates who are subject to the pastor. According to the more rigid theologians, their main duty is obedience.

After Trent, authority becomes more and more concentrated in the bishop and his delegate, the pastor. Where there is a parish school, the pastor becomes responsible for running the school and for hiring and firing the teachers.

Parishes grow larger. By the end of the nineteenth century, the parishes in Paris average 36,000 souls. In many French parishes, it is physically impossible for all parishioners to fulfill their Easter duty. In Germany, conditions are the same. In South America, they are worse, with an average of 50,000 members per parish.

In the United States, the church sets up its parishes according to the European model, as directed by the Council of Trent. It relies primarily on the territorial principle for parish organization. Of course, there are numerous exceptions for national or personal parishes for the growing number of immigrants who speak a common language.

Lay Trusteeism

Toward the end of the eighteenth century and the first half of the nineteenth, the United States' church has to deal with lay trusteeism. The Catholic Encyclopedia defines a trusteeism as "a form of insubordination in which lay parishioners, particularly lay parish trustees, on the basis of civil law, claimed excessive parochial administrative powers, and even the right to choose and dismiss pastors."

The reason for adopting the trustee system in the United States is clearly stated by Fr. Vincent Harold, O.P., in his letter to Rome:

Each church is, by an act of legislature of the state in which it is situated, made a distinct corporation, and this incorporated body possesses all the rights and privileges of a citizen of the States. ... The income of the churches is principally derived from an annual rent which each member of the congregation pays for his seat (pew) in the church .... These pew rents and burial charges are recoverable by law. It was considered an odious and a dangerous thing for the priest to appear in a Court of Justice, as the prosecutor of his flock even for the recovery of just debts. Yet this would sometimes have been inevitable had he been appointed the legal representative of the church property. It was therefore thought prudent that a certain number of the respectable lay members of each church should be elected for these purposes. The Pastor is always President of the Board, and no act of the trustees can have legal force without his signature. To prevent the abuse of power the lay trustees are annually elected. The priest is the only member whom the law recognizes as permanent without election.[15]

Trusteeism had some European roots in the church wardens of Germany and France (*marguillers*). It becomes a problem in the United States' church between 1785 and 1884. It is largely confined to New York, Pennsylvania, and Louisiana. The problem develops from a combination of factors: unruly priests; "old world" nationalist feelings; poor education of the laity; and appeals to civil law to solve property disputes.

The difficulties of the trustee system are often exaggerated by clerical historians who see the problem as a threat to the pyramid of their authority.

Leonard Swidler writes:

In the three quarters of a century of controversy over the trustee system there do not seem to have been much more than a dozen prominent trustee difficulties in all the United States ...[16]

Bishop John Carroll had defended the trustee system, including the right of the laity to have a voice in the appointment of pastors:

Wherever parishes are established no doubt a proper regard

(and such is suitable to our government) will be had to rights of the congregation in the mode of election and representation.[17]

In 1829, the First Council of Baltimore effectively eliminated the problem of lay trusteeism. It ruled that, wherever possible, no church is to be erected without being legally assigned to the bishop.[18] After the First Council of Baltimore, the bishops and priests adopt a more clerical and authoritarian style of parish administration—a style which is largely supported by the peasant and conservative immigrants who pour into the United States at this time. Because of the difficulties with trusteeism, American parishes come more and more under the control of the bishop. They also move further away from the congregationalism of their Protestant neighbors.

The Code of Canon Law

The Code of Canon Law was published in 1917. The canons on the parish basically repeat the parochial principle as laid down by the Council of Trent.

Canon 216, No. 1, states:

The territory of every diocese is to be divided into distinct territorial parts; to each part is to be assigned its own church with a definite part of the population, and its own rector as the proper pastor of that territory is to be put in charge for the necessary care of souls.

Canon 451 lays down the principle that the pastor remains dependent on the bishop. He is responsible "for the care of souls under the authority of his bishop."

Since the publication of the Code of Canon Law, a parish is understood as "a distinct, clearly limited territory and distinct, clearly determined population with its own proper church and its own proper pastor."[19]

Many commentators note that canon law does not define, but merely describes, the parish. Theologians point out that the parish of the Code is based on an inadequate ecclesiology, is exclusively legalistic, and one-sidedly clerical.[20]

Vatican II

Vatican II (1962-65) does not specifically address the theology of the parish. It follows the Council of Trent in describing the parish in a relationship of dependence between the pastor and his bishop:

> But because it is impossible for the bishop always and everywhere to preside over the whole flock in his church he cannot do other than establish lesser groupings of the faithful. Among these, parishes set up locally under a pastor *who takes the place of the bishop* are the most important: for in a certain way they represent the visible church as it is established throughout the world.[21] (Italics mine.)

In its *Decree on the Pastoral Office of Bishops in the Church,* Vatican II does, however, depart rather significantly from Trent's territorial definition of diocese when it states:

> A diocese is a section of the People of God entrusted to a bishop to be guided by him with the assistance of his clergy so that loyal to its pastor and formed by him into one community in the Holy Spirit through the Gospel and the Eucharist it constitutes one particular church in which the one, holy, catholic and apostolic church of Christ is truly present and active.[22]

As is evident in Vatican II's definition, the accent is on the People of God rather than on territory. If this shift from territory to people is applied to the parish "level," many new models of parish become possible. First, however, it may be helpful to review some recent discussions on the theology of the parish.

CHAPTER TWO

A Theology of the Parish

It should be clear now that the historical Jesus left no eternal blueprint for the form of the parish. As a living organism, the church, even at the parish "level," constantly adapts to the changing cultures, situations, and countries in which it lives. There is a continuing osmosis between the church, with its inner, divine life, and the world, the earthly community, within which that life becomes incarnate. The inner life—the Word, faith, grace, charity, holiness, the dynamism of the Spirit—remains the same, but that life becomes enfleshed in various ways in different local "bodies" of church. This process of enfleshment is very much the result of continuing discernment, human imagination, energy, and creativity.

Every believer who responds to the Spirit is constantly shaping the body of the church by his/her faith, holiness, and unique ministries which build up the church. Through the gifts of its members, the church in its external form, is born again in every age and culture.

Insofar as the parish is shaped by the external forces of culture, society, and history, it is subject to study and evaluation by sociology. Insofar as it is shaped by its inner divine dynamism and by its divine mission to the world, it is subject to study and evaluation by theology. For the parish will be a sign or sacrament to the world in the way it takes flesh in any given time and place. It will be an efficacious "sacrament" only insofar as it succeeds in its mission to mediate the Lord's saving grace to the people of a particular time and place. In actual reality, of course, it's impossible to separate the inner and outer life of the church.

On the other hand, the parish can be studied from the viewpoint of sociology or from the viewpoint of theology. Again, the two viewpoints will never be neatly distinguished. The purpose of this chapter, however, is to concentrate on the theology of the parish, leaving sociology to the experts in that field.

Under the broad heading of theology, the parish can also be studied in its juridical aspects, insofar as it is subject to the disposition of canon law. This is the approach used by Von Nell-Breuning and other canon lawyers. It can also be studied in its ecclesial aspects as one form of the mystery of the church composed of the People of God celebrating its ecclesial, liturgical, and sacramental life. It's from this latter perspective that most ecclesiologists reflect on the theology of the parish. The purpose of this chapter is to discuss the parish primarily from the perspective of ecclesiology, leaving the juridical approach to the experts in canon law.

In the final analysis, the parish, *our* parish, will be created by us. It's not a given "from above"; it's not frozen in divine law. Allowing for the mysterious dynamism of the divine elements, the parish is nothing other than baptized believers in a faith relationship to each other. The parish, *our* parish, will be whatever we believers, listening to the Spirit, decide it will be. We can, therefore, experiment with different models, testing, weighing, comparing one with the other. We can submit them to the church's discernment process and then accept them, reshape them, reject them, or create new ones which express ourselves, our times, and our faith in a more authentic way. The form of the parish is a work of art. It is a song, a poem, or a celebration. It is a sign of who we are and whom we are called to become.

In recent years, many models or theories of the theology of the parish have been discussed. It may be helpful to review a few of these before proposing new models for the parish of the future.

The Jerusalem Community

The first model suggested for the parish is the Christian community of Jerusalem: the church is the upper room; James is the pastor; there is a community of believers whose activities are preaching, sacraments and works of charity (Acts 4:32-35).[23]

While the Jerusalem community may be a continuing inspiration to today's parishioners, it can hardly serve as a model for today's parish. James is not like the modern pastor. The Jerusalem community is closer to being the episcopal community of the diocese than the pastor's community of the parish. Besides, territory was not a factor for the Jerusalem community. And, unlike the modern parish, the Jerusalem "parish" had no slack or fallen away members.

Ecclesiola in Ecclesia

A second, more plausible model was suggested by German liturgists (1920-1934). It is often called *ecclesiola in ecclesia,* a small church within the church. The parish is the church in miniature. Like the family in the secular state, so the parish is the basic cell in the universal church. This model is best described by M. Schurr:

> As a collapsible cup is made of separate rings which fit closely into one another and only form a drinking vessel when they are properly assembled, so it is also with the structure of holy Church which consists of four concentric communities constituting the visible organization of our Lord's body. First there is the outermost ring, the unity of the all-embracing universal Church. The second ring is the episcopate: though founded by divine law its concrete form is defined by canon law. The third ring is the parish, also created by the law of the Church. The fourth ring, finally, is the divine institution of the family sanctified by the sacrament of matrimony and itself consisting of individual Christian personalities.[24]

Four criticisms have been leveled against this model. First, it misrepresents the relationship between the pastor and the bishop. There is an essential difference between the parish priest and the bishop. The priest is only the organ and instrument of the bishop. He is only the extended arm of the bishop. He is not a mini-bishop presiding over the parish community in his own right. Rather, he is acting for the bishop who has delegated to him only some of his own functions (preaching, baptizing), but has reserved others (confirming, ordaining) to himself alone. What he has given, he can take back.

Second, this model presents the parish community as standing on its own within the circle of the diocesan church. However, the parish is not a self-sufficient unit. In present theology, it is an incomplete and dependent cell within the body of the diocese. It needs the diocesan church to complete its identity and mission. It looks to the bishop, who in the documents of Vatican II, is presented as the center of unity.

Third, the critics say, it is not correct to say that what applies to the diocesan church applies equally to the parish church. For the parish is only a *partial* realization of church. L. Siemer, D. Grasso, and A. Blochlinger make the case that what can be said about the church as a whole cannot be said about its parts, neither about the diocese nor about the parish.

Fourth, the family precedes the state. It comes first by the very law of nature. The parish, on the other hand, comes after the diocese. It is a subsequent division of the diocesan church. And the pastor comes from the ordaining hands of the bishop, not from the family.

The parish, conclude the critics, cannot be a church within a church.

Y. Congar's Model

A third model for the parish is presented by Yves Congar. He outlines his proposal in two stages. First, he describes how the parish and diocese compare with the family and the civic community. He is careful to point out that this analogy is not of divine law, but only one adaptation of the church to the state.

Man lives in two communities, says Congar. The family provides the elementary necessities of human life; the civic community provides for "more specific development of human life by providing opportunities for man's growth and differentiation by offering job opportunities and by regulating community life by laws and coercion."[25]

The parish is the maternal womb out of which the Christian, as such, is born *sine addito,* that is, without further distinguishing characteristics. He is born into the parish as a baby is born into the family. There his elementary needs are cared for.

The diocese, on the other hand, assigns to the baptized Christian the greater tasks of the church. It places the Christian in the larger public order and engages him in the public work of the church. In so doing, it does for the Christian in the ecclesiastical sphere, what the city or state does for the citizen in the civic sphere.

In his second stage, Congar explains that the parish is a community which is founded by a double dynamic: one "from above"; the other "from below." "From above" come the divine elements of truth, grace, and power. "From below" comes everything that pertains to men and women living in a specific community with each other, interacting in a communion of prayer, mutual service, and apostolic activity. As the parish is formed from below, it also contains smaller groups and communities. It is from these smaller communities that the larger parish community draws life and energy. Congar defines the parish as *the* community.

Theologians have objected to Congar's theory on the grounds that the analogy with the family-state relationship does not provide a properly theological statement on the parish. Furthermore, they feel that to say a Christian is born into a parish without further distinguishing characteristics is an abstraction. Such a situation never exists in real life. Finally, in criticizing Congar, Charles Davis says, "The parish cannot without further ado be said to be a community."[26]

Much of the criticism directed at Congar's model is legitimate. However, his emphasis on the community of the People of God and the dynamic "from below" remain an extremely valuable contribution to the theology of the parish. More about this later.

K. Rahner's Model

Karl Rahner has devoted his considerable talents to an examination of the theology of the parish. His model of parish is quite different from that of Congar. It is also more complex.

For Rahner, the first thesis is that the parish is the local representative actualization of the church. "The Church appears and manifests itself in the event of the central life of the parish."[27] To actualize itself, especially in its sacramental celebrations, the parish needs to be in a place. "The Eucharist can be celebrated only by a community which is gathered together in one and the same place ... All this means that the Church, in its innermost essence, is itself directed to a localized concretization; and this in no way harms or lessens its universal destiny and mission to all men."[28]

In his second thesis, Rahner states that the parish is the *primary* realization of the church as event.[29] For him, the parish is the primary, normal, and original form of the local community because the parish exists by the principle of place alone.[30] The parish is a union of people who live together in a specific place; community is based on the principle of locality.

Rahner builds his model from three elements: 1) the parish as an actualization of the church through the celebration of the Eucharist; 2) the parish as event, again, through sacramental celebration; and 3) the parish as place.

Charles Davis offers a rather convincing critique of Rahner's model. Rahner, says Davis, has given us a theology of community not of parish. Locality can hardly be the principle for a parish because, in the long history of the church, there are just too many exceptions. Then, too, merely living together in the same place does not bring about community. The fact of living together can be divisive, for example, blacks in the suburbs. Further, the parish can hardly be called the *original* form of the local community. It is true that today the parish is the most frequent and usual form of the local community, but "the original form of the local community is rather the episcopal community with priests gathered as a group around the bishop and assisting him to serve the needs of the community."[31]

Finally, Rahner's model, says Davis, carries with it the danger of falling into super-naturalism. It puts too much weight on the celebration of the liturgy as a force for building the community or parish. While the liturgy has a considerable unifying power, it cannot build a community merely by the force of its supernatural elements alone, such as the Word, the bread, and the cup. The liturgy, to be authentic, must also celebrate the people's life in the world, a life of work and service. It must seek to affirm and celebrate the community which is formed by those ordinary *natural* dynamics which bring believing people together. Besides, the liturgy, as such, cannot actualize into community everybody who lives in a particular locality. There remain the aetheists, agnostics, apostates, and people of other faiths. These witness to the pain of division and the incompleteness of the liturgical community. To see the parish only in terms of its liturgical celebration is to separate the parish from its natural life in the workaday world.

Faith is a pre-condition for celebration. The liturgy has no power to gather into community those who do not believe. The liturgy must celebrate the joy and the pain of the human condition; otherwise, it will be unreal, a flight into angelism or supernaturalism.

D. Grasso's Model

In 1959, D. Grasso proposed a model of parish which, to a large extent, has actually been the operative model since the publication of the Code of Canon Law.

Grasso is trying to overcome a purely juridical view of the parish.

He contends that the parish can be the subject of theology only insofar as it is an extension of the diocese. The parish is not a self-contained entity, but one open to both the diocese and the universal church. His thesis is based on the statement of the Council of Trent and the Code of Canon Law that the parish is *a part* of the diocese. The parish, therefore, is only an extension of the diocese and, as such, is essentially a relative ecclesial reality.

Alex Blochlinger criticizes Grasso's theory on the grounds that it is ambiguous. He says Grasso argues from "part" as understood in the geographical sense of the code, to "part" as understood in the theological sense as a supernatural participation in the mystery of the church. Grasso uses the word "part" with two different meanings. Yet he places the theological essence of the parish in the specific relationship of the parish *as a part,* to the diocese and to the church as a whole.

Unless one understands "part" in a mystical sense, Grasso's theology of parish remains largely territorial. It is rather far removed from the new emphasis placed on community since Vatican II.

M. Winter's Model

In 1973, Michael Winter published a book entitled, *Blueprint for a Working Church—A Study in New Pastoral Structures.* He argues that "the standard patterns of parish, diocese and religious order, which we now use, were fixed in the medieval period."[32] The parish and diocese are too large. The present structures do not build community. In the average parish, the mission seems to be serving the structure rather than the structure serving the mission. The structure of the parish, as in medieval Europe, assumes the nation is basically Christian by habit. The parish structure, formed by Catholic Europe, is not designed to respond to today's world. Today's situation is often described in terms like "anonymous Christian," "post-Christian world," "minority Christianity," or "diaspora situation." The parish often is situated in a very secular community where faith cannot be taken for granted. The mission of the church, says Winter, should respond to *today's* situation, and mission should prevail over structure.

Winter believes that the church and, therefore, the parish, "must be a community of worship, charity, witness and apostolate."[33] To achieve this kind of community, both the diocese and the parish must be radically restructured. The size of the diocese must be reduced so that there will not be more than fifty priests for each bishop. Winter believes that, if a diocese is to possess a sense of unity, "it must be in some way a Eucharistic community."[34] It must be able to celebrate the Eucharist together, thus "bringing together the majority of the population."

The size of the parish must also be reduced, says Winter. The basic Christian community should have about twenty or thirty people. The *normal* celebration of the Eucharist should be in private houses with no more than twenty or thirty people present. At regular intervals, all the Catholics of the same town should have one Eucharist. At less frequent invervals, the whole diocese should celebrate the Eucharist with the bishop. The basic community should be built around the "natural social groupings" as they are found in towns, cities, and rural areas.

Winter is quite aware that it's impossible to build small basic communities around the celebration of the Eucharist with the present shortage of priests. For this reason, he calls for the ordination of the natural leaders of these "basic Christian cells." Most of these leaders would, of course, be married men, gifted with natural ability, dedication, and a sense of communication. They would continue to hold regular jobs and minister to their communities on a part-time basis. These part-time priests would be responsible to the fifty full-time priests who would work as pastoral teams overseeing the various sub-units.

Winter's theory has much to recommend it. The emphasis on small community and the centrality of the Eucharist has a long tradition in the church. It has a good basis both in theological and sociological principles.

Perhaps the most obvious difficulty with Winter's theory, however, is the present law of celibacy which prohibits the ordination of married men. Another law prohibits the ordination of women. No doubt, many of the "natural leaders" of these "basic Christian cells" would be women.

A less obvious problem is the relationship between the full-time, overseeing priests and the part-time priest leaders of the base communities. If the part-time priest leaders celebrate the meaningful experiences of the Christian faith in the life of the basic communities, such as baptism, marriage, and death, how do the full-time priests relate to the blood and sweat of the life of the basic community? If they do not relate to the basic communities with deeply human and faith bonds, to what community do they relate? Do they become detached administrators who merely oversee the life of the basic communities but are not a real part of it?

Furthermore, who organizes the town or city apostolate? Who is responsible for articulating and implementing the apostolate of the various basic communities? If the apostolate should flow from the eucharistic celebration, is not an occasional regional Eucharist a rather weak base for the common apostolate? While Winter's theory presents an exciting and attractive ideal, it brings with it a host of organizational problems in today's complex society.

CHAPTER THREE

The Future of the Parish

If restructuring the parish is going to be more than a mere rearrangement of the church furniture, it must, first of all, recover at least the spirit of the New Testament churches. Second, it must take seriously Vatican II's emphasis on community, its basically positive, incarnational view of the world and, finally, its persistent call to responsibility at the level of the local church.

Before suggesting directions for the parish of the future, it may be helpful to reflect on some of the New Testament principles of church and then to review the pertinent ecclesiology of Vatican II.

The New Testament Roots

No one has summarized the principles of community life in the New Testament better than H. Kahlefeld. In a lecture at Innsbruck in 1956, Kahlefeld outlined eight principles of church organization as modeled on the New Testament.

1. The parish community is the Holy Church, the People of God, the salvific community of the Messiah, the family of the baptized living in one specific area, in the midst of the human community of the *Polis*.

2. This community is the bearer of salvation for all [people] with whom Christians form the *Polis*. It gives a public manifestation founded by God and consequently bears a corresponding responsibility.

3. The community lives not only in the assembly place (the church or places of worship) but in the homes of all Christians as well.

4. The celebration of the Eucharist is the most profound source and the highest manifestation of the life of the family of God.

5. The now-neglected "Supper of Charity" (agape) ought to find its continuation in the community members' charitable care of the poor, and extra-liturgically in community gatherings full of a great spirit of brotherhood.

6. On the vigils of Sundays or Holy Days a liturgy of the Word should be celebrated with a reading of pericopes chosen from the Old and New Testament, followed by a biblical homily and a community prayer full of spirit, so that everything serves to nourish the Christian's faith.

7. The pastor is the father of families in his community. As shepherd of his flock he takes care of order in community life and attends to everyone's spiritual and corporal needs, besides being responsible for the conservation and successive passing along of the storehouse of faith and the appropriate celebration of the mysteries.

8. There are various functions in the liturgical assembly subordinate to the building up of the community and to worship, each according to its own kind. Paul says that all are means of action of the Spirit of Christ, which is to say they are charismatic functions.[35]

Vatican II

Vatican II's emphasis on the eucharistic community and the local church comes from two different documents. The first is found in the *Constitution on the Sacred Liturgy:*

> The bishop is to be considered the high priest of his flock. In a certain sense it is from him that the faithful who are under his care derive and maintain their life in Christ.
>   Therefore all should hold in very high esteem the liturgical life of the diocese which centers around the bishop, especially in his cathedral church. Let them be persuaded that the church reveals herself most clearly when the full complement of God's holy people, *united in prayer and in common liturgical service* (especially the Eucharist), exercise a thorough and active participation at the very altar where the bishop presides in the company of his priests and other assistants.
>   But because it is impossible for the bishop always and everywhere to preside over the whole flock in his church, he

cannot do other than establish lesser groupings of the faithful. Among these, parishes set up locally under a pastor who takes the place of the bishop are the most important: *for in a certain way they represent the visible Church as it is established throughout the world.*

Therefore the liturgical life of the parish and its relationship to the bishop must be fostered in the thinking and practice of both laity and clergy: *efforts also must be made to encourage a sense of community within the parish, above all in the common celebration of the Sunday Mass.*[36] (Italics added.)

It is rather significant that this section does not mention territory. The point of departure for the parish community is the liturgical service of the bishop's altar. "The lesser groupings" represent the visible church throughout the world. The principle of organization is not canon law, but "God's holy people united in prayer." "A sense of community" must be encouraged at the *parish* level.

Vatican II's second document which emphasizes the local church is the *Constitution on the Church:*

This Church of Christ is truly present in all legitimate local congregations of the faithful which, united with their pastors, are themselves called churches in the New Testament. For in their own locality these are the new people called by God, in the Holy Spirit and in much fullness (cf. 1 Thessalonians 1:5). In them the faithful are gathered together by the preaching of the gospel of Christ, and the mystery of the Lord's Supper is celebrated, "that by the flesh and blood of the Lord's body the whole brotherhood may be joined together."

In any community existing around the altar, under the sacred ministry of the bishop, there is manifested a symbol of that charity and "unity of the Mystical Body, without which there can be no salvation." In these communities, though frequently small and poor, or living far from any other, Christ is present. By virtue of Him the one, holy, catholic, and apostolic Church gathers together. For "the partaking of the Body and Blood of Christ does nothing other than transform us into that which we consume."[37]

This section stresses the spiritual elements of the church. While the first paragraph refers to the diocesan church, the second certainly refers to the parish. The constitutive elements appear to be the People of God, the Holy Spirit, the Gospel of Christ, and the mystery of the Lord's Supper. Even small communities represent the "one, holy, catholic, and apostolic church."

Ecclesial Principles for the Local Church

It seems evident, both from Scripture and from Vatican II, that any discussion about the parish of the future must begin with the formation of a basic *faith community*. The process of formation will have its divine and its human elements, a dynamic "from above" and a dynamic "from below." Before Vatican II, when the pyramid model of church was dominant, the dynamic "from above" often referred to the hierarchy. In practice, it implied that the bishop would start the parish, send his priest-delegate as pastor, and then continue to control the parish through him.

However, the dynamic "from above" refers more accurately to the spiritual power which brings any faith community into existence and sustains its life. This spiritual power is revealed in the active reigning of the kingdom of God, the Word of God, the Holy Spirit, faith as response, and the sacrament of regeneration. No matter what model of parish is adopted, it must own and nurture its spiritual dynamic "from above."

The dynamic "from below" refers to the very real community which exists as soon as the believer, in communion with his fellow believers, says "yes" to the Word and then commits himself or herself to living that Word as a committed disciple of the Lord. It highlights the individual believers as they live their faith in a particular time, history, and culture. They may be living their faith in a barrio or in the inner city, but that's where their community is, culturally and sociologically. It is formed "from below," right there where believers live their faith.

Every model of community, no matter how small, will need to retain some bond with the larger church. This bond may even be called "hierarchic" and be viewed as one dynamic "from above."

In building the institutional part of the parish, one can place the accent on the hierarchic dimension "from above" or on the culturally conditioned faith response "from below." Before Vatican II, the hierarchic dynamic "from above" received more emphasis than necessary. Since Vatican II has placed a new emphasis of the People of God, on the Word, and on community, it is possible to place more emphasis on the dynamic "from below" in constructing models of the parish of the future. In each case, the new emphasis will be a question of *degree*. It will never be either/ or, but always both/and.

The Dynamic "From Below"

Both Vatican II and the signs of the times call for a new emphasis on the dynamic "from below" in building the parish of the future. At least seven reasons can be listed:

1. The shift toward a more incarnational view as taught by Vatican II, especially in *The Pastoral Constitution on the Church in the Modern World.* The parish, as a living cell of the organism that is the church, is a divine-human reality which, in its outward form, is shaped or constituted both by divine and human elements. *The Constitution on the Church* says these two elements "form one interlocked reality which is comprised of a divine and human element. For this reason, by an excellent analogy, this reality is compared to the mystery of the incarnate Word."[38]

It follows that the concrete form of the parish can never be defined once and for all in permanent, legal, sociological, or theological categories. The human, incarnational element of the parish is part of man's changing self-consciousness and part of a rapidly changing culture and society. If the outward form of the parish is going to be an authentic sign of man's self-awareness and of his faith response within his changing culture, the relationship between the human and the divine element will constantly have to be questioned, reevaluated, and re-shaped. The parish is called to be a sign or sacrament of God's saving grace in human form in *today's* world. B. Kloppenburg says it well:

> Since the church is both immanent and transcendent, it must always be open, and disposed to recommence its incarnation in the new forms and in new historical and cultural contexts, and not link itself exclusively or indissolubly to any race or nation, to any one set of customs, to any particular way of life, old or new.[39]

If the human, external form of the parish is going to be an authentic incarnation, it must be enfleshed by the historically and culturally conditioned believing community. Neither the Jesus of history nor the Spirit of Pentecost has given the church a divine cookie cutter which can be imposed "from above" to shape the outward form of all Christian communities.

Vatican II has acknowledged the positive values in today's culture. In the *Pastoral Constitution on the Church in the Modern World,* we read:

> Because it flows immediately from man's spiritual and social nature, culture has constant need of a just freedom if it is to develop. It also needs the legitimate possibility of exercising its independence according to its own principles. Rightly, therefore, it demands respect and enjoys a certain inviolability, at least as long as the rights of the individual and of the community, whether particular or universal, are preserved within the context of the common good.[40]

Of course, the mystery of evil is still at work in all cultures until the "coming of the Lord." So the church, even at the parish level, needs to exercise its gift of discernment "given to every believer." It needs to sift the wheat from the chaff in its own particular culture. Nevertheless, like the church universal, the parish is called to "recognize" and affirm the positive values within its own culture. In some cases, it may be the Mexican-American culture; in others, it may be a Black culture.

2. The Vatican II shift toward pluralism.   *The Constitution on the Church* plainly blesses "a variety of local churches":

> By divine Providence it has come about that various churches established in diverse places by the apostles and their successors have in the course of time coalesced into several groups, organically united, which, preserving the unity of faith and the unique divine constitution of the universal Church, enjoy their own discipline, their own liturgical usage, and their own theological and spiritual heritage. Some of these churches, notably the ancient patriarchal churches, as parent-stocks of the faith, so to speak, have begotten others as daughter churches. With these they are connected down to our own time by a close bond of charity, in their sacramental life and in their mutual respect for rights and duties.
> This variety of local churches with one common

aspiration is particularly splendid evidence of the catholicity of the undivided church.[41]

In its outward form, the parish is called to witness to variety, not to sameness. While the parish is called to witness to the unity of the church universal, it is also called to proclaim to the world that there is room for the unique human personalities within the Christian community.

3. The need for dialogue with the world.   Since the kingdom of God is greater than the church, the parish needs to be in dialogue with that part of the kingdom of God which is not mediated by the church. The parish needs to build bonds or structures of dialogue with its civic community. The primary purpose of the dialogue is to learn from the civic community how and in what forms the kingdom of God is present there. The parish, like the human person, needs to be dialogic. It needs to be open and vulnerable to the dialogue, which will be structured, at least in part, on the terms of the civic community. Such dialogue should not be structured primarily for conversion, but for *listening* and then learning something radically new about the kingdom of God. For this reason, the dialogue must be structured more "from below" than "from above." The architects of the form of this dialogue will have to be the pastoral ministers of the local church, the parish.

4. The need to practice the principle of subsidiarity.   The principle of subsidiarity was formulated by Pope Pius XI in his famous encyclical, *Quadragesimo Anno*. It states:

> This supremely important principle of social philosophy, one which cannot be set aside or altered, remains firm and unshaken: Just as it is wrong to withdraw from the individual and commit to the community at large what private enterprise and endeavor can accomplish, so it is likewise unjust and a gravely harmful disturbance of right order to turn over to a greater society of higher rank functions and services which can be performed by lesser bodies on a lower plane. For a social undertaking of any sort, by its very nature, ought to aid the members of the body social, but never to destroy and absorb them.

Vatican II, in its *Pastoral Constitution on the Church in the*

Modern World, recommended the principle of subsidiarity to the international community.[42] If the church is to be a credible sign in the world, it needs to practice in its own house the very principles it proclaims to the secular community. It needs to be a visible sacrament of the word it preaches; otherwise, its word will be nothing more than "sounding brass."

No doubt, the implementation of the principle of subsidiarity will go a long way in maximizing the freedom, responsibility, and creativity of the local church. It will also promote human dignity and maturity. At the same time, it will reduce the lay passivity which is still conditioned to look for answers "from above."

5. The need for a more missionary orientation.   The modern parish, in its main patterns, was molded in Europe at a time when everybody was Catholic. In the United States, the parish has been geared to preserve the faith in a hostile, Protestant environment. It has been concerned mostly about serving its *own* parishioners.

Vatican II, however, tells us that "missionary activity wells up from the Church's innermost nature and spreads abroad her saving faith." If the *Decree on the Missionary Activity of the Church* is to become a reality in the life of the church, the parish needs to shift toward a more missionary orientation. The "missions" begin wherever there is a fallen-away Catholic, an agnostic, an atheist, or a non-believer. It is primarily through the local church, the parish, that the church will make contact with its own missionary field.

6. The need for a more ecumenical orientation at the parish level.
In its *Decree on Ecumenism,* Vatican II took a rather firm stand regarding the church's participation in ecumenical work. Vatican II asked the church "to make the first approaches" toward the separated brothers and sisters. Expressing respect and affection for Protestant churches, the same *Decree* lists some of the elements Catholics share with the other churches: the written word of God; the life of grace; faith, hope, and charity; and the gifts of the Holy Spirit. All Christians are called to foster a greater unity among Christians through dialogue and common prayer. Vatican II states:

> In ecumenical work, Catholics must assuredly be concerned for their separated brethren, praying for them, keeping them informed about the church, *making the first approaches toward them.*[43] (Italics mine.)

In November, 1980 the U.S. bishops' Committee on the Parish reminded Catholic parishes of the need to be committed to ecumenism:

"... if a parish is to be genuinely committed to unity of all of God's people, then ecumenism is a necessary undertaking. The parish joins with other Christian churches in expressing their common faith in Christ and in seeking unity. At the same time, with these churches, and with other religious groups, it shares in fellowship and in joint actions, especially those aimed toward human development."[44]

If the ecumenical effort is going to succeed, it will need to begin at the level of the local church, the parish. Hans Kung writes:

The important point is that official moves on a universal or national level are subsidiary. Ecumenical experiences on the local level should be our *starting point and aim*. The aim is not a giant, universal united Church but a church liturgically, theologically and organizationally diverse—above all, a church that serves the community ...[45]
        Ecumenical union should not grow into a "super institution" or "super church" but into brotherliness with the world.[46]

Basically, if there is no ecumenism in the home parish, effective ecumenism does not exist.

7. The need to develop basic Christian communities.   Perhaps the most exciting development regarding church "from below," since the close of Vatican II, is the rapid emergence of basic Christian communities. The idea of forming basic communities received considerable official encouragement during the Latin American Conference held in Puebla, Mexico, in February, 1979. During this conference, the Latin American bishops gave their wholehearted support to the formation of these basic communities:

It is evident that small communities, above all the BCC, encourage stronger interpersonal relationships, acceptance of the Word of God, review of life and reflection upon reality in the light of the Gospel. They accentuate one's commitment to family, work, neighborhood and local community. We wish to point out with joy that the multiplication of these small communities is an important ecclesial fact and is 'a hope of the church' ... Christians united in the ecclesial basic community deepening their adherence to Christ, seek a more evangelical life at the heart of the community. They work together to question the selfish roots of consumer society, and bring to light the vocation of communion with God and with their brothers and sisters, by offering a valuable starting point in the building of a new society—a civilization of love.[47]

In 1972, Karl Rahner gave his support to the ecclesiology of basic Christian communities. In his book, *The Shape of the Church to Come,* he devotes a whole chapter to "The Church from the Roots." He writes:

The Church of the future will be one built from below by basic communities as a result of free initiative and association ... The Church will exist only by being constantly renewed by a free decision of faith and the formation of congregations on the part of individuals in the midst of a secular society bearing no imprint of Christianity.[48]

Rahner clearly recognizes the validity of the dynamic "from below." Since the Council of Trent, the Catholic Church, in its pastoral practice, has assumed that the local church, the parish, must be started by the bishop. However, there has been a considerable variation in the actual practice of forming the local church. Catholics have often taken the initiative in asking for the establishment of a parish in their own territory.

Rahner moves this dynamic "from below" one step further when he says that the local community has the right to have its community leader recognized through ordination. He writes:

When, however, such a community exists, coming from below, formed through the free decisions of faith of its members, it has the right to be recognized as church by the episcopal great Church and to have its community leader recognized by the great Church through ordination, as long as he can fulfill the necessary functions ... If the Church, in a concrete situation cannot find a sufficient number of priestly congregational leaders who are bound to celibacy, it is obvious and requires no further theological discussion that the obligation of celibacy must not be imposed.[49]

Regarding ordination, Rahner suggests that the community itself should present to the bishop "a leader who comes from among themselves and has the necessary qualities for leadership ..." He says that such a leader "rightly receives ordination" even if he is married.

In the United States, the National Federation of Priests' Councils has given considerable support to the formation of basic Christian communities by publishing a booklet entitled, "Developing Basic Christian Communities." The NFPC is also conducting workshops to help pastoral ministers set up basic Christian communities.

The theology of the basic Christian community has rather solid foundations in the New Testament in the churches of the Pauline letters. It seems to be a rather logical development of incarnational theology and of the ecclesial dynamic "from below" which were encouraged by Vatican II.

From the viewpoint of theology, there is no reason why the ecclesiology of the basic community could not be adapted to the American church. It is true, as Karl Rahner says, that the Christian community must be organized around the celebration of the full Eucharist. It is part of the Roman Catholic tradition that a Christian community gets its life and its mission from the celebration of the full Eucharist. A model of the local church without the Eucharist will not survive as a Catholic model.

I find it hard to believe that the official church will long ignore the requests of these basic Christian communities to have their own ordained eucharistic presiders, married or single. The good of the local church has priority over the ecclesiastical law of celibacy.

Needless to say, the leader "with the necessary qualities for leadership" could very well be a woman. If so, the whole church, in prayerful discernment, will have to decide whether, in selecting its eucharistic presiders, it should give priority to sex or to "the necessary qualities for leadership."

In conclusion, there are no preformed models for the parish of the future. From the viewpoints of theology, history, and culture, the whole situation is too fluid and too changeable to limit the parish of the future to a specific number or kinds of models. As more Catholics internalize the ecclesiology of Vatican II and respond to the Lord's Word and the Spirit he sent, they will engage the gift of discernment and the unique creativity with which they were blessed. They will then build and shape the parish of the future so that it will respond both to the new calls of the Spirit and to the needs of their own time and place.

PART TWO

Questions and Answers
for Parish Councillors

FUNDAMENTAL CONCERNS

"The structures for participation can take many forms, but the parish council remains the most promising way to make sure such participation occurs."

The Parish: A People, A Mission, A Structure
(A Statement of the Committee on the Parish).
National Conference of Catholic Bishops, November, 1980

Choosing Council Members

Q How should council members be chosen? Is it right for the pastor and one or two of his favorite parishioners to pick them?

A No. Council members should be chosen by the people of the parish through an annual election. My book *The Practical Guide for Parish Councils* (Twenty-Third Publications) gives a step by step procedure for conducting council elections.

Briefly, you need to set up an election or nominating committee. This committee, composed of six or eight persons who have experience on councils and who know the parishioners, will first draw up a list of qualifications for candidates. Then they will select a list of nominees, preferably by personal interviews. If the pastor isn't on the election committee, the list of names should be presented to him for review. He may very well have useful information which the committee doesn't have.

After the committee has reached a consensus on a list of candidates, it should decide on the form of the ballot and the method of holding elections. Many councils allow only registered parishioners to vote.

After the votes have been counted, the chairperson of the committee should announce the results and the date for installation of council members. Some constitutions allow the pastor, after consultation with the council, to appoint two or three members to the council to achieve better representation among women, youth, etc. But the number of appointees should be kept to a minimum.

Length of Membership

Q *Our constitution says that "members may not succeed them-*
selves." What's the reason for that?

A Many council constitutions limit the members' tenure to two
or three years. Putting a time limit on the length of service
prevents the growth of a clique and forces the nominating committee to recruit new blood. In this way, the council will have the
benefit of constant rotation of new members, and also of new
ideas.

Besides, service on the council is a form of adult education.
Such adult learning experiences should be offered to everybody in
the parish. The council, after all, exists not for itself, but for the
whole parish.

Planning Ahead

Q *We continue to spend most of our time reacting to the crisis*
of the moment. We never plan ahead, never take a good
hard look at the larger issues. Have you found anything to circum-
vent this situation?

A Many diocesan pastoral councils have a committee for planning and research. Some dioceses even have an office with a
full-time staff.

Parish councils could take their cue from these dioceses and
also set up a permanent committee for planning and research. This
committee could have a sociologist, an historian, a theologian and
an educator. The task of this committee would be to rise above the
nitty-gritty, to ask the big questions, to look into the future, to
study tomorrow's needs, and to plan accordingly.

This committee could well be linked with diocesan and city
planners. It would try to relate the Gospel and the mission of the
church to the changing needs of its own community.

Parish Goals and Objectives

Q *Our biggest problem is that we have no parish goals or ob-*
jectives. How do we go about developing a parish plan?

A The lack of a parish plan seems to be a rather common problem. Some councils don't even become aware of the problem until it's time to approve the annual parish budget. Still worse, some councils actually vote on their budget without any reference to a parish plan.

There are, of course, different models for developing a parish plan. I would like to recommend the following, taken from the Guidelines of the Archdiocese of Newark:

1. Develop a commitment to planning. (A prayer and study day or weekend could help in this development.)

2. Define the parish mission.

3. Gather pertinent information:
   a. Parish data—such as size, personnel, facilities, financial resources, talents.
   b. Basic assumptions (areas over which the church has no control)—such as demographic information, ethnic situation, employment, socio-political development, theological development.

4. Identify areas of concern.

5. Identify areas of accountability.

6. Study possible goals. (Invite total parish involvement at this point.)
   a. Assess needs.
   b. Analyze problem areas.

7. Set goals.
   a. Reduce possibilities to a manageable number.
   b. Determine preferences.
   c. Establish priorities.

8. Set objectives—steps toward achieving goals.
   a. Establish possibilities.
   b. Reduce possibilities to manageable number.
   c. Determine preferences.

9. Develop programs to achieve objectives.

10. Implement the parish plan.

11. Gather and evaluate feedback.

Launching Council in Stages

Q Some members of our steering committee think we ought to launch our parish council in stages; for example, the finance commission, the first year; the Christian service commission, the second year; and so forth. But, some of us think we should start all commissions right away. Who is right?

A I would vote for your side. I'm not sure your side will be right in every case, but my experience has been in your favor.

If the council is to grow into a mature Christian community sharing responsibility for the total mission of the parish, it is important that all the commission chairpersons become true partners in a simultaneous development. This will build a mutual understanding and tolerance right from the beginning.

Besides, to start with only one commission tends to give too much emphasis to the work of that particular commission. Your council could start off so lopsided that it would take years to achieve a proper balance.

Each new commission would have to contend with the older commissions for its own equality and proper status in the council. The first commission could easily tend to "lord it over" the inexperienced new commissions. This would be especially dangerous if you started with the finance commission, which often gets more emphasis than it deserves.

The first goal of a council is to grow into a closely-knit Christian community. The opportunity to grow together is an extremely valuable experience in the whole process of developing a good parish council.

Key Ingredients for Success

Q We are just starting our parish council. In a few words, what are the key ingredients for a successful parish council?

A A tough question to answer "in a few words." I'll limit myself this time to a *few* of the "natural" ingredients of a good parish council.

Since God became human, the human is the apt vehicle for the divine. St. Thomas Aquinas tells us that grace builds on nature.

For this reason, successful parish councils pay special attention to the principles of any good organization. Fr. Gerard Egan has outlined a few of these principles in *The Parish in Community and Ministry,* edited by Evelyn Whitehead and published by Paulist Press (Ramsey, NJ 07446). His "human" organizational principles can easily be applied to parish councils:

"1) Members must know what human *needs* they are trying to meet through the formation of community." For instance, councilors need companionship, community, and intimacy.

"2) Members formulate general or wide-ranging statements of *mission* (containing) the values, theology, and philosophy of the community." For a parish council, the mission statement articulates the vision of the parish community. This vision provides the broad context within which the ministries of the parish community will work.

"3) Members establish concrete, specific, behavioral, measurable, and obtainable *goals* and objectives that are adequate translations of mission statements." In the council meeting, the mission statements become concrete. They take on flesh. The council determines the kinds of ministries which help achieve the mission and the vision of the parish community.

"4) Members design step by step *programs* to achieve each goal and objective." In the parish council system, programs are designed by the appropriate committees.

"5) Members acquire the working *knowledge* and *skills* needed to execute these programs efficiently and effectively." Goodwill is not enough. If councilors themselves do not have the expertise and training to carry out the program, they will need to rely on the competence of the full-time staff members of the parish.

"6) Members see to it that whatever *resources* beyond working knowledge and skill are needed to execute programs are available at the time they are needed." Thus councilors, through their committees, may have to provide books, meeting rooms, and transportation to get the job done.

"7) *Structure.* Members divide up the tasks of the community in ways that best serve the needs of members and in ways that promote the fullest participation of members." Councilors learn responsibility only if they really assume responsibility. They witness to their commitment or non-commitment by the way they carry out the tasks of parish council.

"8) *Relationships*. Members have a clear idea of what to *expect* of themselves in terms of the tasks of the community and of what they might expect of one another." In many councils, it might clear the air if the members were to write down a list of their expectations. What does the pastor expect of the councilors? What do the councilors expect of the pastor?

"9) The members communicate with one another, especially for:
  A. information sharing
  B. feedback."
Councilors need to build a climate during council meetings in which it is easy for members to offer feedback to each other.

"10) Members know, understand, respect, and use effectively such basic principles of human behavior as reinforcement, modeling, and shaping in pursuing the goals of the community." The council meetings should be a time when the members support and affirm each other in their various ministries.

"11) *Climate*. Members cultivate an open community in which free and informed choice is normative." In view of the Gospel, the council needs to respect the freedom of choice for all its members. The council cannot enforce a kind of militaristic obedience.

"12) *Environment*. Members know how this community affects and is affected by other social-cultural systems in the environment." The council needs to be sensitive to the neighboring parishes, both Catholic and Protestant. It needs to be aware at all times of the strain, stress, and movements within the civic community where the parish is located. The more the council can connect with its neighboring communities, the more effective it will be in carrying out its mission."

Parish councils could pause now and then to evaluate themselves in view of these organizational principles. Faith, prayer and goodwill are important ingredients. However, they do not eliminate the need for natural common sense.

Approving the Constitution

 Q *Should the whole parish be invited to approve the constitution of our parish council?*

A Yes.

However, I would suggest you propose the "constitution" as *Experimental Guidelines* for the first three years. This will present a more flexible stance, a greater openness to suggestions from the parishioners. The first three years will be a period of trial and experiment. Guidelines can easily be modified as the council gains experience. To many people, the term "constitution" conveys a rigid, legalistic image.

The whole parish should have an opportunity to review and discuss the guidelines. This is all part of the educational process. To by-pass the parish at large is to invite apathy toward, or rejection of, the council.

One of the key goals during the formation period is to build as many relationships as possible. If the council is to be an effective organism (not organization), it has to be sensitive to the changing conditions in the whole parish. This can be achieved only if living relationships are fostered and sustained. The guidelines can serve as the introductory handshake offering friendship and involvement to all.

Setting Priorities

Q *Should the parish council or the commissions set the council's goals? If the commission sets the goals, should the parish council approve each commission's goals?*

A The whole parish council (all voting members) should set the goals. The individual commissions have to relate their functions and goals to the total parish apostolate and then adjust their priorities accordingly.

No commission should develop its goals in isolation from the other commissions of the council. To do so would be to nullify the main purpose of the council, which is to coordinate *all* parish activities. If one commission can force its priorities on the rest of the council, then the tail is beginning to wag the dog. The council must remain the chief policy-making body in the parish.

Authority: Commissions or Council?

Q *We have a problem regarding the flow of authority between commissions and the councils. Our finance board wants the ultimate decision on how different programs are to be financed. My idea was that the finance board was to work out a budget with all the other boards on the council and then present it to the parish council which approves, modifies, or rejects it. Unless we do it this way, we will have two decision-making bodies. I would like your honest opinion.*

A The elected parish council normally is the only policy and decision-making body. The finance board with its financial experts serves the council. The board does all the homework, prepares the budget, and submits it to the elected council members. The councilors will then evaluate the budget in the light of the goals and priorities which they have established. They may see a need to shift the mission of the parish and may adjust the budget accordingly.

The boards make recommendations to the council. They do the necessary research to document and support their recommendations, but the council makes the final decision. As you indicate in your question, the decision-making authority remains with the elected members, not with the board members whose services were enlisted because of special expertise.

Pastoral Rewards

Q *During a recent continuing education program for the priests of the Diocese of Youngstown, I conducted a brief survey regarding their experience with parish councils. In one question, I asked: "What aspects of the parish council experience have you found the most rewarding personally?"*

A Here are some of their answers:

—The interest and involvement of the laity.
—The initiative and cooperation of the people on the council working in the lay ministry for the good of the church.
—Discovering how willing the laity are to shoulder responsibilities because of their lay ministry.

—The fact that the people do want to share in the pastoral ministry of the church. They know their capabilities and their limitations.

—Getting closer to the people. I appreciate the feedback the council brings from the people in the pew, from the celebration of the liturgy to mundane repairs. It helps me to exercise better leadership in the parish. I believe councils are an effective tool for shared responsibility.

—Talking on an equal level with the members of the council.

—Seeing the whole parish represented.

—Realizing the basic faith and honesty of God's people.

—Seeing our liturgy committee grow.

—Giving the council members a better insight to the working of the parish and its problems. It introduces them to the concept of ministry.

—More lay people being involved and becoming more informed about the general parish operation.

—Working together to meet the needs of the parish through input, discussion, and shared decisions.

—Our council never got off the ground because of a bad experience when we tried to introduce it.

—The enthusiasm of the people for lay ministry.

—The lay involvement and the sense of shared responsibility in the parish.

—The enthusiastic response of the people now undergoing formation.

—The success of consensus decision-making.

—The way our people accept responsibility and share it.

—The success our committees have had in exercising their initiative and in giving freely to express the personality of our parish.

—Coming closer as a Christian family.

—The involvement, participation, and growth experience on both the part of the people and the clergy.

—A better functioning community.

—Better communications.

—My deeper awareness of the needs of the parish and, vice versa, the parish's recognition of the needs of the staff.

—A more effective witness of the parish community to the larger civic community.

How Parish Organizations Fit

Q *We have spent the last three years: 1) studying the decrees of Vatican II, 2) restructuring communities of neighborhoods, and 3) running training programs for neighborhood couples. The diocese has just sent guidelines for parish councils which are very loose. Since no other parish in our diocese has a structure such as ours, with trained people, we are somewhat unique. We have the basis for democratic representation of our 2,300 families. How do we represent organizations, such as C.F.M., Y.C.S., C.Y.O., and the Rosary and Holy Name Societies? Will it become unwieldy with grassroots and societal representation?*

A *The Constitution on the Church* and *The Decree on the Laity,* which your people have studied for three years, form the best foundation for a good parish council. Your careful preparation is truly unique. I hope you build your council on that foundation.

I agree that your parish council could become unwieldy if you tried to represent all the parish societies. A parish council is not an amalgamation of existing parish societies. With all your grassroots preparation, it would be a mistake if your council became weighted in favor of existing parish societies.

I would, first of all, suggest a survey of your parish to find out what percentage of your parishioners really belong to these parish societies and what their average age is. Less than ten percent may belong. Second, find out why the rest of the parishioners don't belong to your parish societies. Third, with help of the officers of your societies, conduct an evaluation of the goals of these societies in the light of Vatican II's teaching on the apostolate. After you have gathered enough facts, you may know what direction to take.

Representation on the council should be based on service to all the People of God. Identification with a parish society does not automatically qualify a parishioner to offer the best service to all the People of God in the parish. Parishioners share in the priesthood of Christ and the saving mission of the church in virtue of their baptism, and not in virtue of paid-up membership in a parish society.

So, I would suggest that you do not bypass the election process by simply appointing representatives from your parish societies. Elected members may resent this. Besides, it would not be a good application of *The Constitution on the Church.*

I would suggest that your nomination committee place the names of some society officers on the election ballot. Then the whole parish will have a chance to "discern their charisms" and to choose their services for the "upbuilding of the church." If parish society officers are elected, they will feel they have earned their seat on the council like everyone else.

Shared Decision-Making

Q As a pastor, I feel we're playing games with this business of lay involvement. We talk one set of rules; we play another. Laypersons today are too well informed, too well educated, and too caring for us to toy with them.

For instance, a few months ago we held a diocesan meeting to discuss the need to increase our parish assessments to inner-city schools. Only the pastors *met with the bishop; only the* pastors *decided the issue. No representatives from our parish councils were present, nor were they consulted.*

We speak one way; we act another. It all adds up to much talk and token gestures. If parish councils are supposed to share our responsibility, why do we continue to by-pass them when really important decisions are being made?

A Your question answers itself: parish councils should not be by-passed in any regional decisions. Excluding them from such decisions does indeed reduce "shared responsibility" and "shared ministry" to a game of words. It also contributes to the growing credibility gap between laity and bishops. If this practice continues, more and more lay persons will soon be "too busy" to serve on parish councils.

Your question also reveals some of the pain we all experience in living and working in a human, sinful church. It's not easy to accept the ambiguity of the earth-bound church which "is always in need of reform" (*Decree on Ecumenism,* 6). The church (and that includes all of us) proclaims one message and practices another. Too often it is a poor servant to the Word it proclaims. That's why we confess "that we have sinned through our own fault ... in what we have done, and in what we have failed to do."

In the past, we priests often promoted a view of the church that was unreal and ethereal. We did this by overemphasizing the holy, divine, and sacred elements in the church. In its official documents, Rome also built up an image of a holy, sinless church. It was fond of sacred titles and issued its decrees and declarations through *Sacred* Congregations and through the *Holy* Office.

The Sacred Congregation isn't really more sacred than your parish council whose members are all consecrated by the holy chrism of baptism. And the Holy Office isn't any holier than the church office at St. Cunegunda's.

Yet we are all to blame insofar as we accept an exaggerated divinization of "holy mother church." We may do it because we would rather bask in the aura of the divine than take our rightful place in the ranks of sinful, struggling humanity. We would rather remain children and assume that a divine and holy mother is making divine, holy decisions for us. That's easier than accepting our own adult responsibilities in the difficult and fallible process of discerning the Father's will.

With the emergence of parish councils, we need to be more honest about the warts on the face of "mother" church. In council retreats, we need to prepare the councillors to live and minister in a human church, burdened with the sin of all its members, including priests and bishops.

On the other hand, once we have confessed our sin, we ought to repent and do something about it. In your case, you could write a letter to the presidents of the priests' senate and the diocesan pastoral council. Then, at their next meetings, they could discuss your problem openly and honestly. In this way, you could help your diocesan church close the gap between the postconciliar theory and preconciliar practice. You would also be exercising your prophetic ministry in calling the church to repent and reform. Both priests and laity will find it easier to minister in a church which owns up to its mistakes and learns from them.

Handbooks and Guidelines

Q *Our steering committee has collected many parish council handbooks and guidelines from various parts of the country. Some of us would simply like to adopt one of them, cut out all*

*the discussion, and get started. But others object. They say we
don't need any handbooks or guidelines at all. What should we do?*

A Handbooks and guidelines can serve a useful purpose. If
they are endorsed by the bishop, they at least indicate the extent to which he supports the parish council idea. It is encouraging to know that the bishop is willing to risk an experiment in new parish structures. Diocesan guidelines will bring some kind of unity into the various parish councils in a given region. This will make it easier for parishes to work together in common apostolates.

However, diocesan guidelines can also create some special problems. The first problem arises when guidelines don't fit into the unique local conditions of a particular parish. Diocesan guidelines can hardly provide for the wide diversity of the parishes in a given diocese. If parishes are too literal in applying such guidelines, they build up a new legalism which actually obstructs the pastoral effort. They use the guidelines to hang themselves.

The second problem pertains to the people. How will guidelines affect the people who use them? Will the guidelines respect their freedom? Will they help people grow in Christian responsibility?

For their own growth, the people need to be challenged by a wide range of options. Rather than force external conformity, guidelines should strive to win the internal consent of the parishioners. This requires a certain sensitivity to the unique personality of each councilor.

This is the heart of the problem: how can guidelines "guide" and still leave people free for personal growth? It would be easy to publish very specific rules and regulations for parish councils. Many Catholics would actually prefer this. It's easier to relate to things than to people. Guidelines could reduce people to objects by formulating detailed rules to solve problems. This would avoid that painful, direct encounter of one person with another. This would "manage" the situation. Of course, it would also eliminate the risk, the pain, and the joy of Christian living.

One pastor stated emphatically that the lay people need detailed regulations. "We have to lead them by the hand," he said; "Otherwise, they won't move at all."

This may be true in a minority of cases. Some Catholics may

still wish to be treated like children. They may be afraid to accept the risks and dangers of adult responsibility in the church. But surely, such immaturity should be challenged, not perpetuated.

For these reasons, guidelines need to be *painfully* vague. They should have enough loose ends so that a wide variety of people can identify with them. At the same time, they should stimulate a creative response.

Guidelines may never become ends in themselves. They may not presume to structure the Spirit in the church. Before the Spirit, all guidelines are under judgment.

Yet, there has to be some order in all human relationships. We are, after all, quite human. So normally, we will have doubts about our own ability to know the will of the Spirit. We need to wait for the discerning judgment of the larger community of believers. Sometimes, this will be the parish. Other times, it will be the diocese. Thus, guidelines which truly reflect the teaching of the larger church can deliver the individual from the vagaries of the passing whim.

It hardly needs saying that guidelines should take their inspiration from the Gospel and the teaching of Vatican II. They should, therefore, be eschatological. That is, they should witness to the pilgrim nature of the church. They should have that tentativeness which is a mark of openness to the changing signs of the times. They should be evaluated on a regular basis and amended according to changing needs.

Advice or Authority?

Q   *Our pastor insists that our parish council is "only advisory." He leaves no doubt that we have no ultimate authority. All of the council's decisions, as well as those of the committees, can be overruled, even if they have been made in faith, prayer, and good conscience. As a result, we can't get people to run for election. How do we deal with this problem?*

A   This problem has often been discussed. As is evident, it's a problem that won't go away soon. It reflects a theology which is deeply imbedded in the life and practice of many pastors. Perhaps a little history will provide a better perspective for understanding the pastor's attitude. The problem may not be all his fault.

Since Vatican II, most pastors are less legalistic in their pastoral styles, but the principles of canon law and jurisdiction still carry a lot of weight. These principles mold attitudes and condition pastors. While that's not all bad, it's not all good either.

Canon lawyers tell us that, historically, Roman Catholicism is dependent on the ancient Roman law which, to a large extent, has shaped canon law. Roman law was the product of the *imperium* form of government. *Imperium* means "the right or power of commanding." It is essentially a government in which all power "comes down from the top." In democracies, of course, the power "comes up from below" through election by the people.

Roman law is basically family law. In the family model, the father has all the power and all the jurisdiction. He even has power of life or death over his children. When a baby is born, he decides if it will live or die.

The mother, in the Roman system, has the authority. Power and authority are distinct and different. While the mother has no power and no jurisdiction, she has authority which must be consulted. When the father is away from the home, the mother has the authority to run the family. Legally, she has the responsibility for the children *who are minors.*

In the Roman system, the children have no rights. They are objects in the care, or the custody, of the mother.

In ancient Rome, this family model became the basis for the Roman government. The father became the emperor with all the power and all the jurisdiction. The mother became the senate with the authority to be consulted and to give advice. The child became the citizen. He/she was "cared for" by the senate. During some periods before Christ, the citizen didn't even have the right to vote.

From Constantine (305-337) to Pope Gregory VII (1073-1085), the Catholic Church gradually absorbed much of the Roman system: the pope became the emperor, with all the power and all the jurisdiction; the bishops became the senate, with the authority to be consulted; the laity became the citizens, who were minors "to be cared for."

Of course, contemporary bishops also have the power of jurisdiction. However, even to this day, when the pope calls a synod of bishops (every three years) it has only a consultative voice. In Vatican II's *Constitution on the Church,* the laity are still called "children" and "sheep" who "are cared for" by the bishops and priests. They are described as having "the right ... to *receive spiritual goods from their sacred pastors.*" Diocesan pastoral councils, composed mostly of laity, have only a consultative voice. (In actual practice, many bishops share some decision-making responsibility with diocesan councils.)

The ancient Roman family model is still very much with us. In some parish councils, today's laity experience this model as condescending paternalism. They are treated like children, as if they had no authority of their own. Even the "authority" to be consulted or to give advice is considered to be a delegation of the authority of the pastor who can give it or take it away. The nature and exercise of authority is part of Vatican II's unfinished business.

I have taken the position that councils should be decision-making within the boundaries of faith, morals, liturgy, and general and diocesan law. I feel the ministry of the council can't be separated from the apostolate of the church. And the apostolate of the church flows from the *decision* of the Lord's baptized disciples who, in a very personal way, have given their *decisive* "yes" to the call of the Word. They are now living out that decision in the apostolate of the council. Sharing in the apostolate of Christ means more than giving advice; it means saying "yes" to the call to die for the Lord so that his mission, his apostolate, may be accomplished. True discipleship includes a disposition, an ongoing decision, to be martyred. In the apostolate, the disciple's neck, not his advice, is on the line.

To "deal with your problem," I suggest you adopt the consensus decision-making system. After you become comfortable with it, your "advisory only" status will be just so many words in your constitution. You can live with that until you get a new pastor.

Consensus Decision-Making

Q   *What do you mean by consensus decision-making? We hear the phrase used more and more in council circles, but we don't know what it means or how it works.*

A   It's difficult to understand consensus decision-making simply by reading about it. Usually, councillors learn consensus decision-making by *experiencing* it, with the help of a skilled facilitator.

It may be useful, however, to offer a brief introduction to some of the main features of the system. What follows is adapted from suggestions contained in *The 1973 Annual Handbook for Group Facilitators,* published by University Associates, La Jolla, California. Some suggestions deal with attitude or preparation; others, with the process itself.

A. Preparation:

In the decision-by-consensus process, each councilor is asked to:

1. Prepare his or her own position as well as possible before the meeting but to realize that the task is incomplete and that the missing pieces are to be supplied by the other members of the council; to do this well, he or she has to have the agenda at least ten days before the meeting.

2. Recognize an obligation to express his/her own opinion and explain it fully, so that the rest of the council will have the benefit of all the members' thinking.

3. Recognize an obligation to listen to the opinions and feelings of all the other members and to be ready to modify his/her own position on the basis of logic and understanding.

4. Avoid conflict-reducing techniques such as voting, compromising, or giving in to keep the peace and to realize that differences of opinion are helpful; in exploring differences, the best course of action will gradually make itself apparent; compromise begins only when members are ready to modify their positions.

B. The Process:

A number of suggestions can be made about how consensus can be achieved:

1. Councilors should avoid arguing in order to win as individuals. What is "right" is the best collective judgment of the council as a whole, as a *community* of faith.

2. Conflict on ideas, methods, solutions, and so forth, should be seen as helping rather than hindering the process of reaching consensus.

3. Problems are solved best when individual councilors accept

responsibility for both hearing and being heard, so that all council members are included in what is decided.

4. Tension-reducing behaviors can be useful so long as meaningful conflict is not "smoothed over" prematurely in an effort to keep the peace.

5. Each councilor has the responsibility to monitor the processes through which work gets done and to initiate discussions of the process when it is becoming effective or ineffective.

6. The best results flow from a fusion of information, logic and *emotion*. Value judgments about what is best include members' feelings about the data and the process of decision-making.

In using the consensus system, some elementary courtesies should also be observed. Councilors should avoid "politely" masking a statement as a question: "Don't you agree that ...? or "Wouldn't you think ...?" In phrasing a "question" in this way, the asker is actually seeking approval of his/her statement. Such questions hinder rather than help the process.

Also, councilors should not introduce their comments by saying: "You probably won't like this but ..." or "I know this might not sound like a good idea but ..." They should not prejudge the reaction of the members or undercut the value of their own input.

The process moves along better if councilors get in the habit of *owning* their statements by saying "I" rather than "We" or "They" or "One." When one councilor includes the others in his/her statement, those others may feel compelled to disassociate themselves from the statement. That's not always easy to do. Besides, it wastes precious time.

Consensus decision-reaching should be an aspect of shared ministry. It should be carried out in a context of Christian collaboration, of co-laborers in the same vineyard. H.B. Karp offers three guidelines for the collaborative approach in consensus decision-reaching:

1. "Only individuals who are competent to contribute to the outcome (of the process) should be included."

2. "Only those individuals in the decision-making process who, in

some way, will be responsible for the outcome should be included." In other words, they should not "pass the buck" when decisions backfire or draw flak from some parishioners.

3. "Only individuals who freely wish to collaborate should be included." Out of reverence for the Christian's individual freedom under the Gospel, collaboration can't be forced or dictated. Even collaboration must be the free gift of a lover.

Implementing Conference Recommendations

Q   *Our parish council voted to send me as a delegate to the Detroit "Call to Action" Conference. What can our council do now to implement the recommendations of that conference?*

A   First, your council can devote a special meeting to a careful study of the Conference's final papers. At this writing you can obtain copies by writing to: Origins, The National Catholic News Service, 1312 Massachusetts Ave. N.W., Washington, D.C. 20005.

The Detroit Conference was part of the Catholic bicentennial celebration. It was sponsored by the National Conference of Catholic Bishops. Entitled "A Call to Action," the Conference discussed the following eight general topics: 1) church; 2) ethnicity and race; 3) family; 4) humankind; 5) nationhood; 6) personhood; 7) neighborhood; and 8) work. The 1,340 delegates came from all over the United States. Responding to the bishops' "call to action," they offered more than three hundred recommendations for action. The recommendations were grouped under the eight general topics of the Conference.

Many of the recommendations are well beyond the competence of the parish council. Such topics include the ordination of women and the elimination of sexist language from Catholic publications, among others. These are being evaluated by the National Conference of Bishops.

To deal with the other recommendations, your council needs to adopt some kind of "sifting" process. Here is one possible approach. You might label all the recommendations according to the "level" of implementation. There are at least five such levels: 1) parish; 2) diocese; 3) American church; 4) the church universal; and 5) the church and civic or government agencies.

After your council has decided which recommendations belong at the parish level, you could assign the recommendations to the appropriate council committees, i.e., liturgical matters to the liturgy committee, educational matters to the education committee, and so forth. Your council could then set up *ad hoc* committees to deal with those recommendations which do not fit under any of its standing committees.

Here are some examples of recommendations that can be implemented by the parish council:

1. That committees for political responsibility be designated at parish levels.

2. That there be a commitment to quality education for all students so they might enjoy meaningful work and life-styles.

3. That we unite with papal and episcopal teachings in calling for a prayerful, critical analysis and a transformation of structures causing social injustice.

4. That we evaluate church property every year and divest ourselves of whatever is unnecessary.

5. That Catholics in all sectors of the church cooperate with other groups in their communities to recognize the dignity and sacredness of each person, committing themselves to establishing deep respect for all life.

6. That the church eliminate sexual discrimination.

7. That the structures to insure participative decision-making by the Catholic community (including parents, students and educators) be established or strengthened to determine total Catholic educational policies at the local level.

8. That efforts be made to evaluate the effectiveness of the religious education of Catholic students attending public schools and that the improvement of these programs be constantly pursued.

9. That Catholics, as citizens, participate in the policy-making bodies that govern public schools.

10. That the parish community educate itself in its role of

"neighborhood servant" and implement this commitment by these or other methods:

a. By reaching out to inter-faith and neighborhood coalitions.

b. By participating in parish-based diocesan programs.

c. By initiating programs to meet specific local needs not met by other groups.

d. By committing its spiritual, material, and personnel resources to this mission, even to the extent of funding a parish coordinator of social ministry.

Installation of Councillors

Q *Have you heard of any paraliturgical ceremonies for the introduction of new members into the parish council?*

A One parish in Michigan recently celebrated a "liturgical installation" at a special Sunday Mass. The new councillors were seated in the first pews for the Liturgy of the Word. After a brief introduction to the theme of the liturgy, the lector read 1 Corinthians 12:12-31 for the epistle. "The body is one and has many members, but all the members, many though they are, are one body ... if all the members of the body were alike, where would the body be? ... You, then, are the body of Christ. Every one of you is a member of it. Furthermore, God has set up in the church, first apostles, second prophets, third teachers, then miracle-workers, healers, assistants, administrators and those who speak in tongues."

The Gospel was taken from Mark 4:3-9. "And other seeds fell into good soil and brought forth grain, growing up and increasing and yielding thirtyfold and sixtyfold and a hundredfold."

After the Gospel, the new councilors came forward and stood around the altar. The pastor then addressed them as follows:

Service to God's people takes on many forms; yet no matter what the form, it demands a total gift of self. As a Christian community we have a responsibility to be a sign of kingdom of God in this city. Christ calls us, as his disciples, to forgive sinners, feed the hungry, clothe the naked and proclaim the Gospel to the poor.

The apostle Paul reminds us that all service in the church is a fellowship of ministry. You men and women who stand here today have been chosen by the people to become partners in God's fellowship of ministry. Let us pray that God may bless your ministry and that it may build up the church of God.

Priest: Our help is in the name of the Lord.

People: Who made heaven and earth.

Priest: Let us pray.

Oh, God, our Father, look down upon us today and send forth your Spirit to bless and strengthen these our brothers and sisters who are offering a special ministry of leadership in our parish council. Make them sensitive to your Word and to the needs of this parish and community. Give them courage to seek your truth and your will in all things. Give them the grace to fulfill their unique roles in the priestly, prophetic, and kingly mission of Christ. We offer our prayer through Jesus Christ our Lord who lives and rules with you and the Holy Spirit, God forever and ever.

People: Amen.

After this prayer, each new councillor came before the pastor who placed his hands in theirs, saying:

I welcome you into our fellowship of ministry to the people of God in St. Mary's. May God bless our labors in His vineyard in the name of the Father, and of the Son, and of the Holy Spirit.

Councillors: Amen.

The homily explained the implications of the many diverse gifts God has given to all the members of the body that is the church.

The Prayer of the Faithful mentioned each new councillor by name and asked for God's blessing and guidance for each one. The new councillors remained standing around the altar until Communion time when they received under both forms. After Mass, the new councillors recessed with the priest while the people sang: "God Gives His People Strength." After Mass, the parishioners were invited to meet the new councillors and to share coffee and donuts with them in the parish hall.

The pastor reports that this paraliturgical ceremony has helped the people understand the seriousness of serving on the council. At the same time, it has raised the council above the level of "just another committee" and given it the prestige and visibility it deserves.

Policy or Administration?

Q *During the last meeting, we spent two-thirds of our time discussing the janitor's neglect of school maintenance. Then in twenty minutes, we rejected a proposal to hire a full-time CCD director. Some of us are getting disgusted with the overemphasis on picayune administrative details. We rarely have time for liturgy, family life, and CCD problems.*

A Many parish councils seem to have similar problems, especially in their first year of operation. Sometimes, this happens because council members fail to distinguish between policy and administration. Other times, lay people, who lack sufficient Christian formation, simply are not aware of the Lord's system of priorities. Then, too, some councils need stronger leadership from the chairperson. A carefully prepared agenda also can be helpful.

Let's take up the question of priorities at greater length. "Should we pave the parking lot or should we upgrade the CCD?" "Should we buy stained glass windows for the church or should we raise the teachers' salaries?" "Should we adopt a mission parish in South America while we still have a large debt on the school?" The list of questions is endless; each one raises the problem of priorities.

Needless to say, we have no neat little "handbook of priorities" from the Lord. On the other hand, the value system of the parish does not evolve solely out of the feelings or whims of particular council members.

Some priorities come to the parish church from the larger diocesan church. Some come directly from Christ. Other priorities "happen" here and now because the parish community is incarnate in a specific city, in a particular time in history. These are the "signs of the times" or the circumstances of the human condition.

Vatican II, in the *Constitution on the Church,* tells us that certain priorities flow from the very nature of the divinely established church. The first priority given to the church is to proclaim the saving news of the Lord. Second, the church has the mission to build community, "to establish among all peoples the Kingdom of Christ and of God." Third, "the liturgy is the summit toward which the activity of the church is directed." Fourth, the church, like Christ, exists "to serve and not to be served."

Vatican II frequently teaches that the purpose of the church is to extend the priestly, prophetic, and kingly missions of the Lord "until he comes again."

So, it seems that all parishes, since they are the church in miniature, need to solve priority problems in the light of the total mission of the Universal Church. No parish is an island unto itself. Parish council decisions need to relate to the priorities of the diocese and of the community.

No discussions of parish budget should really begin until all councillors have arrived at some common understanding of goals and priorities. Such understanding can hardly be achieved without a serious process of formation into the mind and nature of the church. Some good program of Christian formation may be necessary. This could prevent long hours of arguing about administrative details.

Apart from the more or less objective priorities which come from the church, there is a wide variety of subjective or local needs which require the attention of the council. A constant inventory of needs, through surveys and study committees, will help determine these priorities. Once the list of local needs has been established, it seems the problem of the janitor and school maintenance could be dispatched rather quickly.

Pastor Appointees

Q   Recently, we had our first election to form a parish council. We elected eight members. But after the election was over, we suddenly discovered that the pastor, on his own authority, appointed seven others to the council. Two were trustees. The other five represented parish organizations. Those of us who were elected object to the idea of having such a large number of appointees with equal voting rights.

A   I agree that seven is a rather large percentage of appointees. Since American Catholics are conditioned by the democratic process, they believe firmly in the elective system and resent appointments to the council. For this reason, every appointment needs a clear justification in the minds of councillors.

Appointments increase because parishes are trying to bridge the gap between the old and the new system. Once parish councils function effectively, trustees and some old parish organizations may discover they can offer their services to the council without continuing as separate organizations.

It would be a mistake to view the council as an organizational linkage of existing parish organizations. It would also be a mistake to make appointments to a council just to keep various organizations happy.

Appointments should be few. They should be based on the principles of representation and service. Many elections do not seat a sufficient number of women on the council. So the principle of representation may require the appointment of women. Other times an important skill, such as education, isn't represented. Then the effectiveness of the council in serving the parish is seriously hampered without a special appointment.

Regarding the two trustees, some parish councils simply appoint two members of the administration committee to serve as trustees.

When you draw up your guidelines, set a limit to the number of appointees—two or three at the most.

Steering Committee Needed?

Q *Our pastor thinks we should set up a steering committee to start our parish council. Why can't we skip all the fuss of a steering committee and get on with the parish council right away?*

A It really doesn't pay to skip any steps in starting a parish council. It may take more time, but the steering committee is the best way to go.

Generally, the pastor appoints the steering committee. He selects people who represent all segments of the parish—old and young, joiners and non-joiners, men and women.

First, the steering committee educates itself. It studies Vatican II's *Constitution on the Church* and *The Decree on the Laity*. It discusses the diocese and the parish.

Second, the steering committee launches an educational program for the whole parish. It collects a good supply of materials. The education of the parish could include the following:

—series of sermons
—bulletin inserts
—a filmstrip during the Sunday Masses
—an open parish forum conducted by the steering committee
—open discussion during the meetings of all existing parish organizations
—neighborhood discussions in various sections of the parish, conducted by the steering committee members
—outside speakers from the diocesan office or from other parish councils in the area
—a parish survey of special talents and areas of interests.

Third, the steering committee develops interim or tentative guidelines for the parish council. It collects copies of guidelines from other dioceses or parishes and adapts them to fit its own needs. At this stage, guidelines are broad and flexible. They simply define the nature and competence of the council and give the number and kinds of commissions. They provide direction for the parish and educate the parishioners so they'll be informed when they vote in the first election.

Finally, the steering committee sets up the procedures for the first elections. It determines eligibility to vote, qualifications of candidates, the list of nominees and, finally, the form of the ballot. It decides whether the voting will be done by mail, at special meeting, or during Sunday Mass.

In many parishes, the steering committee takes a hard look at all the parish organizations. It reviews their purpose and membership. After a thorough evaluation, it determines how the organizations fit into the council's commission system.

Steering committees may take six months to a year to prepare for the formation of a parish council. When the council is elected, the steering committee is dissolved.

Accountability for Council Decisions

Q   *I'm the pastor of a large city parish. I feel the bishop, if he really supports the council idea, should hold the whole parish council accountable for decisions which prove unwise and harmful. Too often, the bishop calls only the pastor, reproves only the pastor, and holds only the pastor accountable. In case of dif-*

ficulty, the bishop should summon at least the council chairperson along with the pastor. That would be one way of showing us that he really takes parish councils seriously. What do you think?

A As Ann Landers says, "Thanks for writing." I couldn't agree more. Most pastors are quite aware that they have the major responsibility for running the parish. They don't mind taking their share of the heat. But they resent the fact that the laity, who are also responsible for a bad decision, get off scot-free. If shared responsibility is for real, it means: share the glory, *share the grief.*

Limiting Members' Terms

Q As a pastor, I feel a three-year term is too short. Just when the councilors are getting to know what the parish and council are all about, their term is up. Besides, it's a lot of bother to train new members all the time.

A Most council constitutions limit the members' term to two or three years. Councils do better when they are forced to look for new blood and new ideas. They also avoid the appearance of being the pastor's clique or an elite in-group. Besides, after three years most councillors need a break, either to devote themselves to other apostolic works or to become re-acquainted with their families.

It may indeed be some "bother" to train new members. But the council is an experience in adult education which should be offered to everyone in the parish. It's also a training center for lay ministries. It's a school for growth in faith, prayer, and holiness. Training new members is the council's most important business.

Reappointments to the Council

Q If a person is elected to the council and completes his three-year term, may the pastor re-appoint him to another three-year term?

A Some constitutions require a year of absence from the council after completion of a three-year term. They don't allow members to succeed themselves either by election or by appointment. Others allow two three-year terms before requiring an absence of one year.

With due deference to your constitution and your local situation, I hope the pastor doesn't appoint a person who has just completed a three-year term. The council shouldn't become too dependent on one member. Otherwise, when that person dies or moves, the council may fall apart.

Whether we minister as pastors or as councillors, it's not good pastoral practice to make anyone dependent on ourselves. Councils, like the church itself, should be built on "no other foundation" than "Jesus Christ" (1 Corinthians 3:11).

Parish Secretary as Member

Q *Our pastor always appoints the parish secretary as a voting member of the council. Some of us feel the secretary should serve the council without being a voting member.*

A Often councils elect one of their own members to serve as secretary to the council. He or she may give the minutes to the parish secretary for typing and mailing. Sometimes councils ask a willing parishioner to perform that service.

However these details are handled, the council should be free to decide who will be the secretary to the council. Appointments to the council should be kept to a minimum. Both pastor and council should honor and respect the vote of the parishioners. While the parishioners may have nothing against the parish secretary, they did not, in fact, elect him/her to represent them on the council. The secretary should, of course, never be appointed to the council without the prior consultation and approval of the full council. They can then decide if the secretary should be a voting or non-voting member.

Automatic Voting Membership

Q *We have hired a full time youth minister in our parish. Does he automatically become a voting member of the parish council?*

A No.
Automatic membership on the council should be rare. The

democratic process, while not absolute, should nevertheless be respected. The people of the parish should have their say about who represents them on their council.

The youth minister could, of course, become a member of the youth commission, if the council has one. In this way, the council and the parishioners will have a chance to evaluate his leadership qualities. If their judgment is favorable, no doubt they will be happy to vote him a seat on the council.

MEETINGS AND VOTING

Proxy Votes

Q   *Why can't I ask any knowledgeable person to vote in my place when I'm absent from a council meeting?*

A   The parish council is a deliberative, not a legislative assembly. *Robert's Rules of Order* says that proxy voting "is unknown to a strictly deliberative assembly, and is in conflict with the idea of the equality of members, which is a fundamental principle of deliberative assemblies."

The right to vote comes with membership on the council. And councillors can't give their votes to others any more than they can give their membership to others.

Besides, more and more councils are shifting to consensus decision-making. They put less emphasis on the vote. Instead, they emphasize the process of debate and discussion which leads to the vote. A councillor cannot be part of this deliberative process unless he's present. Naturally, such a process sometimes stretches out over several meetings.

Electing a Chairperson

Q   *Our constitution requires the whole parish to vote for the election of the chairperson. Most of the parishioners don't even know the candidates. So they vote off the tops of their heads or they don't vote at all. What do you think of this system?*

A   I suggest you amend your constitution. Council members should elect their own chairperson. They are in the best position to know who is gifted with the skill, the charism, to expedite the process and business of the meeting. Besides, they will be more disposed to cooperate with the chairperson. Democracy can be overdone.

Right Setting for Meetings

Q   *Could you say something about the physical arrangements for a parish council meeting? We frequently meet in the parish hall, and it's cold, drafty, and uncomfortable.*

A I have visited many parish council meetings, so I have some feeling for your problem. I have attended a meeting held in a gymnasium where the people sat for hours on wooden folding chairs at long tables. It was difficult to see and hear the councillors at the other end of the table. At another meeting held in the basement of the rectory, there was no ventilation. Sister kept wincing as clouds of blue cigar smoke slowly, ever so slowly, moved past her face.

Another time, the pastor kept going and coming, answering phones or doorbells. Each time he returned, the chairperson patiently reviewed the discussion for the pastor's benefit. Other members were visibly irked by the constant repetition.

Competition for the best meeting room can get rough in some parishes, but I believe the council should have more status than Boy Scout Troop No. 89. Many rectories are large enough to provide a comfortable setting for a council meeting. Some effort should be made to provide a conference table arrangement with comfortable chairs.

Needless to say, acoustics are important. If the Legion of Mary is saying the Rosary in the next room, separated only by a movable partition, the councillors may be edified, but they won't hear the discussions.

Surely, a secretary could answer phones and doorbells during council meetings and refer only emergency calls to the priests.

Some council member could arrive thirty minutes before the meeting to attend to the details of physical arrangements. A beverage break would go a long way to make the meeting a pleasant and joyful experience. A little extra attention to details like these can make the differences between success and failure.

Parishioners Interrupt Meeting

Q During our last council meeting, almost all our time was taken up by visiting parishioners. Without waiting for recognition from the chairperson, they frequently broke right into our discussion. Everything was disorganized. How should this be handled in the future?

A   In my visits to parish councils, I have observed many different styles of leadership. Sometimes it seems that chairpersons are so concerned about being informal, open, and unstruc-
tured that they exercise no leadership at all. In a recent meeting
which I attended as a silent observer, there were thirty-nine interruptions from visitors while four elected members spoke only once.

The solution is stronger leadership by the chairperson. A
well-prepared agenda is the first and most important step in exercising good leadership. Such agendas should allocate some time (maximum ten minutes) for comments from visitors.

If elected members have no more status than interested
observers, they will soon resign. Presumably, elected members have
spent considerable time gathering data and preparing themselves to
discuss the items on the agenda. If their homework is not recognized, they will soon stop doing it. Besides, they were elected
because the people thought they had something positive to contribute to the decisions of the council.

Some special attention to the seating arrangement of the
council members might also contribute to proper order. Councillors should really face one another, not the audience.

To establish good rapport with the parishioners, the council
could hold an annual open forum for the while parish. This is a
non-business meeting designed to gather information and to take
the pulse of parish community. It's a time for any and all visitors to
speak their piece.

Study-Time Before Voting

Q   *In the parish council, we often vote off the top of our heads.*
The chairman frequently calls for a vote before we have had
enough time to study the question. What should we do about this?

A   This seems to be a rather common problem. The desire to
participate in the policy decisions of the parish has not produced an equal desire to do research and homework.

To foster intelligent voting, you could mail the agenda to the
council members at least two weeks before each meeting. The agenda could be sufficiently descriptive to indicate the complexity of the
problems. It could include fact sheets, background papers, and pertinent bibliography.

No doubt there are times when you need to invite outside resource people to tackle the more complicated questions. At other times, you may have to appoint *ad hoc* committees to study specific problems. In any event, councillors could refuse to vote on issues when they aren't prepared to do so.

Parish Staff Vote

Q *We have ten full-time staff members in our parish. Each staff person gets a vote on the council. Some of us don't think that is right. I'm heading up a committee for the revision of our constitution. What should we do about this large "staff" vote?*

A I'm not much in favor of the voting system. The consensus system, in which there is no vote, would eliminate, or at least reduce, your problem.

More important than the actual vote is an effective system for getting staff input into the decision-reaching process. In some councils, staff persons serve on the council's standing committees. In this way, their expertise is available at an early and very important phase of the decision-reaching process. In other councils, staff persons are invited to serve as resource persons to the council in the area of their competence, be it liturgy, education, or activities. Since the parish is paying good money for the gifts and special skills of a trained staff, the council should get maximum benefit from them.

Each council has to work out its own relationship to the parish staff. Naturally, it should not see itself in an adversary role. Rather, it should work toward a mutually enriching and cooperative relationship which maximizes the gifts, both of the staff and the councillors.

Time Limits

Q *Is it better to set a limit on the length of meetings, or should we let them run on for four hours, leaving everybody disgruntled?*

A Meetings should not last longer than two hours, including time for prayer and Scripture reading. If your meetings regularly go on for four hours, I suspect one or more of the following is happening:

1. Councillors are not prepared. (No advance agenda, no fact sheets, and so forth.)
2. The council is getting lost in details which should have been discussed and *settled* in the committee meetings before the council meetings.
3. One or two talkative members dominate all the discussions.
4. The chairperson is weak and abdicates his responsibility for keeping the discussion on the agenda.
5. Council committees are not meeting or are not preparing *brief* written reports.
6. Meetings do not start on time.
7. Meetings are too social. (Cocktail gossip and such.)

Meetings can be a pain, but they can also be a joyful sharing in each other's faith and gifts of the Spirit. We should at least *try* to imitate the early Christians: "And day by day, attending the temple together and breaking bread in their homes, they partook of food with glad and generous hearts, praising God ..." (Acts 2:46-47).

Comments from Non-Council Members

Q In our council meetings, there's no receptivity to the other members of the parish who want to voice their concerns. Can't there be at least fifteen minutes to hear the comments of any interested parishioners?

A Some council agendas allow ten minutes for comments from non-council members. That's one way the council tries to keep in touch with the needs of the whole parish.

Other councils conduct an open forum twice a year to hear the concerns of all the parishioners. Such forums are especially helpful when a serious topic, such as closing the school, is being discussed.

During the actual council meeting, it's up to the chairperson to put a time limit to interventions from non-voting members. A ten minute slot early in the agenda should be enough.

A council meeting is a *deliberative* assembly. Duly elected members have come together to conduct the official business of the parish. A council meeting isn't the same as a town hall meeting, so it should not turn into a grand free-for-all. When that happens, meetings drag on and on. Everybody gets bored and frustrated.

Then, too, chairpersons need to respect the vote of the parishioners. If, after an election, a defeated candidate ends up at the council meetings with as much voice as the elected members, voting parishioners will feel as though the election results have been betrayed. Then they won't bother to vote in the next election. The vote has no meaning if anybody can end up on the council.

Finally, most parishes have one or two "characters" who have a great need to talk, to blow off steam. Such chronic talkers can effectively obstruct the deliberations of the council and sorely try the patience of the voting members. The chairperson has to be firm, limiting the outside talkers to the ten minute slot on the agenda. Filibuster by council members is bad enough; by non-members, it can be disastrous. Elected members may decide they are "too busy" to be used as an audience by chronic gripers.

Improving Council Meetings

Q   *After our council meetings, some of us gather at the nearby bar to chat about the meeting. At this time, we hear a lot of complaints about the way our meetings are conducted. Yet the meetings don't get any better. How can we improve our meetings?*

A   You don't give me any clues about what's wrong with your meetings. All kinds of good books are available to help improve meetings. You might consult: *Making Meetings Work* by Leland Bradford or *Taking the Meetings Out of the Doldrums* by Ronald Lippitt and Eva Schindler-Rainman. Both are published by University Associates, Incorporated, La Jolla, California, 92037. *Making Meetings Work* contains numerous forms for evaluating and improving your meetings. They "may be duplicated without special permission from the publisher for free distribution to meeting members."

Here is a sample of *Postmeeting Reactions Form* taken from Bradford's book:

Directions: Please rank-order each statement in each set from 1 (most like) to 10 (least like) to describe the meeting and your behavior. Use this procedure: In each set, first identify the statement you would rank 1, then the one you would rank 10, then 2, then 9—alternating toward the middle of the scale.

The meeting was like this:
( ) There was much warmth and friendliness.
( ) There was much aggressive behavior.
( ) People were uninterested and uninvolved.
( ) People tried to dominate and take over.
( ) We were in need of help.
( ) Much of the conversation was irrelevant.
( ) We were strictly task-oriented.
( ) The members were very polite.
( ) There was much underlying irritation.
( ) We worked on our process issues.

My behavior was like this:
( ) I was warm and friendly to some.
( ) I did not participate much.
( ) I concentrated on the job.
( ) I tried to get everyone involved.
( ) I took over the leadership.
( ) I was polite to all.
( ) My suggestions were frequently off the point.
( ) I was a follower.
( ) I was irritated.
( ) I was eager and aggressive.

Forms such as these can be completed in a few minutes at the end of the meeting. They can then be summarized and openly discussed at the next meeting. Such forms encourage all participants to assume full responsibility for the quality of the meeting *before* they get to the corner bar.

Split Vote

Q   Until now we have had no complaints about our religious education director. Recently, however, our parish council found out that he is an "ex-priest." Immediately, about half the council members wanted to fire him. They brought this matter up during a council meeting, even though it was not on the agenda. The discussion got rather emotional and very personal. Finally, the chairperson called for a vote. It was a tie: seven to seven.

Since the council couldn't come to any agreement, the chairperson asked the pastor to "take care of it." So now it's on the pastor's desk. No matter what he does, half the council won't like it. What do you think about this whole situation?

A It's a sticky one, all right. The pastor is being asked to pick up the pieces after the council has botched it. He can hardly be blamed for letting the whole thing cool off on his desk for a while.

Most council guidelines wisely restrict the council to *policy-making* decisions. When councils get into administrative matters, they are over-stepping their competence and authority. Council members are not parish managers or administrators. The council is not an administrative board. Firing a religious education director is an administrative decision. As such, it is outside the competence and authority of the council.

Your council needs some education about its role and function so that it doesn't get into areas where it doesn't belong. It could also stand a lesson in shared ministry so that it won't pass the buck to the pastor when the going gets rough.

By the way, in my parish council class, your chairperson would flunk as chairperson. First, he allowed this issue to be discussed, even though it was not on the agenda. Second, he called for a vote, even though the council had not studied the issue, was in an emotional state, and was obviously divided right down the middle.

If I were the pastor in your parish, I would probably let the issue rest on my desk for a while until the council's emotions had cooled down. Then I would take the issue to the education commission, listen carefully to their recommendations, and then make my *administrative* decision.

Selecting Topics for Meetings

Q In our council we spend an awful lot of time discussing matters which I feel do not have to be decided by the whole council. How do we get a handle on this problem?

A You need an agenda committee and a strong chairperson. The agenda committee decides what items should or should not be discussed by the full council. Some items should be discussed and *settled* in the council's committees. Other items are the administrative responsibility of the full-time staff, that is, the pastor, maintenance personnel, religious education director, and so forth. Still other items, like one parishioner's chronic complaint, should be handled on a one-to-one basis outside of council meetings. It's the agenda committee's responsibility to make sure that only policy matters get on the agenda. At the same time, the committee must be careful not to lose control or to manipulate the meetings.

After the full council has agreed to accept the agenda, it's the chairperson's responsibility to keep the council's discussion sharply focused on the agenda. Most councillors are "secretly" grateful for a strong chairperson who is time conscious enough to keep the meeting moving. Such chairpersons show that they value the councillors' time by refusing to waste it. They are models of responsible stewardship of God's precious gifts.

Watching Time and Topics

Q   *We spend half of our meeting time hearing about problems concerning finance, administration, and building repairs. It's boring us to death.*

A   For the next three meetings, keep pad and watch handy. Log the time spent on each item on the agenda. Then, armed with the facts, bring this issue to the attention of the full council. In doing so, you will help all members to assume responsibility for the process of your meetings. You will remind them that time, like money, is valuable and that you are concerned about how it is spent.

Liberating the Council Secretary

Q   *I feel that whoever is elected secretary (invariably a woman) is really disenfranchised. Since she is so busy with minutes, she has little or no opportunity to take part in the discussion. She can't even vote intelligently.*

A   Since I have just finished my own term as secretary for board meetings, I have some feeling for your problem.

More and more councils are asking the parish secretary (who is not a member of the council) to take the minutes. Some councils ask any willing parishioner to perform this service. That way all voting members are free to participate in the discussion.

Involving At-Large Members

Q *What do you do when some council members, especially at-large representatives, have no specific tasks or responsibilities? They seem to lose all interest. They just sit there waiting for the meeting to be over.*

A There should be no dead weight on the council. No doubt, your at-large members have been blessed with many unique gifts and talents, so ask them to serve on the standing committees which correspond to these talents. If this doesn't work, invite them to serve on the first *ad hoc* committee you set up, whether it be the elections committee or the workshop planning committee, etc. There does not need to be any conflict between representing at-large constituents and serving on specific committees.

Staff Representation

Q *We now have nine staff members on our pastoral team. According to our constitution, they all have a vote on our council. We feel such a large staff vote overwhelms the rest of the council. The staff can win on almost any issue. In view of the large number of "official" votes, we feel the people of the parish do not have adequate representation.*

A In the United States, the principle of representation gets more emphasis than it deserves. St. Paul, in his letters, is much more concerned about function and competence than about representation.

A careful reading of 1 Corinthians 12, Romans 12 and Ephesians 4 reveals Paul's functional approach to the church. He lists pastors, evangelists, teachers, prophets, exhorters, healers, helpers, interpreters, administrators, and others. All are offering services or doing *functions* which build up the church. If a specific service does not build up the church (speaking in tongues), then it's useless (1 Corinthians 14:28). Naturally, all these functions are open to Jews, Greeks, Romans, males, females, blacks, youth, and senior citizens.

Paul does not build up the church merely by getting representatives from differing classes of people. He is interested, not so much in hearing diverse opinions, as in supporting diverse functions. In fact, he opposes any caste approach to the church. "There is neither Jew nor Greek, there is neither slave nor free, there is neither male nor female" (Galatians 3:28).

I believe, therefore, that the principle of function or competence is more important than the principle of representation. For this reason, I think that all full-time ministers in the parish deserve a vote on the council. I am assuming that all full-time ministers offer a useful function or competence to the up-building of the parish community.

I'm also assuming there is no such thing as a "staff" or "official" vote. In other words, full-time ministers would be expected to have different opinions. They would vote differently, depending on the issue. I'm assuming further, that staff members also represent the parishioners, especially their faith, their needs, and their concerns.

Also, it would be better if you didn't place so much emphasis on the actual vote. (After all, it isn't a question of winning or losing.) You might consider adopting the consensus system. Under this system, it makes little difference whether it is a staff or a non-staff member who moves the council toward consensus.

Then, too, you might check your attitude toward the staff. Do you see them as the "collective boss" against you, the people? Or are they fellow council members who, like yourselves, discuss the issues in view of the Gospel and the good of the whole parish?

The presence of the staff during the council meetings brings about a mutual learning process. The staff learns to listen to the elected members and the elected members learn to listen to the staff. Both groups learn and grow through this dialogue and communal discernment.

Female Presidents

 I don't think women should be president of the council; they are too easily manipulated by the pastor.

A One can hardly make such generalizations on the basis of sex. If manipulation is the name of the game, I suspect women can play as well as men. I don't know if anyone is keeping score; however, after twenty years on the parish scene, I have the distinct feeling that housekeepers and mother superiors take home more trophies than pastors.

Of course, the parish council is no place for manipulation, by men or women. Council meetings should be models of faith, love, trust and respect for the freedom and dignity of all the sons and daughters of God. Willful manipulation is a sin against the Christian community. All Christians are called to serve, not to dominate.

Every council should honestly evalute its own internal dynamics at least once a year. This can be done rather simply by asking each council member to answer the following three questions in writing: "What did you like best about this meeting? What did you like least? What suggestions do you have on improving our meetings?" If the members do not sign their names, it will be easier to distribute the completed sheets at random to the council members for subsequent discussion. The answers to the questions will reveal the feelings of mistrust or manipulation. If the council members are afraid to deal with these sensitive matters directly, they can ask an outside facilitator to perform this service. He or she can more easily diffuse the emotionalism of the issue and maintain a more objective climate.

Representing the Majority

Q   *I worry that I am not well enough aware of the opinion of other parish members and, therefore, might fail to properly project the majority view at our council meeting. How do I overcome this difficulty?*

A   It's important, of course, to be sensitive to the opinions of the parishioners. However, you are not merely representing the opinions of the parish during council meetings. You have your own unique gifts, insights, and grace of discernment. You bring these to the council meeting and offer them to the church. *You minister before you represent.*

On the other hand, the value of your presence at the meeting is considerably increased if you tap into the gifts and resources of your fellow parishioners. Make sure to get the agenda two weeks before the meeting. Then call ten different parishioners before each meeting. Ask their opinions about the items on the agenda. Select some people who seem to have special experience or expertise regarding the items on the agenda. Then ask them if they have any suggestions for future agendas. Make notes and report the results of your phone survey at the meeting.

Some councils take an annual parish survey about liturgy, adult education, and other topics. While such surveys aren't the same as a parish vote, they can provide very useful information for the council's decision-reaching process.

Parish Elections

Parish-Wide Voting on Issues

Q We have a very small parish. Our council wanted to hire a Youth Minister in cooperation with our two neighboring parishes. We could not afford to hire him by ourselves.

We had several meetings with the councils of the other two parishes to work out his job description and to figure out what percentage of his salary each parish would pay.

Everything was going well. But then, during one of our own council meetings, one of our members said that hiring a Youth Minister was such an important decision that the whole parish should vote on it. In fact, he announced he would resign if the whole parish didn't vote.

Our council decided to have the whole parish vote. The final vote was in favor of hiring the Youth Minister. But the vote was very close. Now the parish is divided right down the middle. We have a real conflict situation with strong feelings on both sides. In retrospect, I feel we should never have asked the whole parish to vote on this issue. What do you think?

A I agree. The council represents the whole parish, but it is called to be a decision-making body in its own right.

More often than not, it's a mistake to ask all the parishioners to vote on the decisions of the council. The average parishioners don't have enough information. Nor do they have the time to study the issue. And if there is no opportunity for that give and take which brings about a reconciliation of the different points of view, the vote may be little more than an emotional response.

The decision-making process should stay within the council. It's easier for a small group to argue, to discuss, to reconcile differences and arrive at a consensus.

There is an important distinction between a poll or survey that gathers opinions and information and a ballot that decides an issue. Surveys can be taken to find out where the parishioners are at. They may reveal that the parish as a whole is ignorant or misinformed about a certain issue. They may mean that the council needs to launch an educational program to inform the parishioners about liturgy, social justice, or other issues.

When taking a survey, be sure the parishioners do not see it as a vote which binds the council. The survey form should have a clear reminder: *For information only. Not a binding vote.*

There may be times when a council, in view of its prophetic role, has to make a decision which would not get a majority vote from the parishioners. This is often the case in matters which pertain to social justice and to racial and sexual discrimination. In these areas especially, a parish vote is more likely to reflect the values of the secular culture than those of the Gospel.

I'm sure you have learned something from your experience in hiring your Youth Minister. I hope your council will devote at least some of its time to healing the division in your parish. One of the ongoing functions of a parish council is to build up the unity of the Christian community.

Registered Parishioners Only

Q We have about a hundred families who are not registered in our parish but who come regularly to Mass here. Should they have at-large representation on our council?

A No.
Council members should be selected from the registered parishioners. They have committed themselves to the parish such as it is. They have a prior claim to represent *their* parish.

Poor Voter Turnout

Q Recently, we had an election for our parish council. But the pastor did not prepare the people. Only twenty-two percent of the parish voted, so the pastor has the same old clique he had before.

A Without a doubt, considerable advance preparation is necessary to achieve maximum parish participation in an election. This is a common mistake—pastors who are impatient to launch a council by-passing crucial steps in the educational process.

It's true that apathy will always be with us. And maximum

involvement cannot be achieved easily. The more successful elections usually show considerable preparation through a series of sermons, bulletin inserts and small group meetings. In one parish, a steering committee conducted a series of meetings in the homes of parishioners until the entire parish had been covered.

If the elected council is to be truly representative of all the people in the parish, priests and parishioners need to work together to build a broad base of support.

Right Time for Elections

Q I am looking for a good way to get more people to participate in the elections of our parish council. I have tried sending out ballots by mail but many never come back. I have done it during the Sunday Masses but some people feel the liturgy is no time for elections. I am still looking for a good system.

A Without eliminating ballots by mail or Sunday bulletin, I feel elections connected with Sunday liturgy will produce the largest response. It's true that some people may object to this "secular" intrusion upon the sacred liturgy. However, selection of various ministries in the Christian community is not secular. The activities of the parish council should flow from the eucharistic celebration. They become secular only when they are separated from the liturgy.

However, the election itself should be carefully integrated into the liturgy. Thus the pastor might choose special scriptural readings for that Sunday. St. Paul's letter on charisms in the church would be a good start. The parable about the talents might make a good Gospel selection. The homily and prayer of the faithful would then develop the meaning of election and ministry in the church.

Counteracting Parishioner Indifference

Q Ever since I was assigned to this parish, I have tried to get all the parishioners interested in the decisions and activities of the parish council. So far I have had no success. All our meetings are open to all members of the parish. But, in spite of frequent invitations through parish bulletins, no one shows up. Most of the parish continues to ignore the council.

A It may take some years before the average Catholic pays much attention to the parish council. Many parishioners may be doubting Thomases. They may be skeptical about the council's real authority and its decision-making role. Some may suspect that it's just another committee, with no real voice in a rather rigid church system. Others may be conditioned to passivity by many years of "Father knows best." Still others, for a variety of reasons, have simply narrowed their religion to the moral minimum of "Sunday Mass." An attitudinal survey of the parishioners might reveal still other reasons for apathy toward the parish council.

However, a pastor can upgrade the image of the parish council. In a variety of ways, he can show that the parish council is a real sign of the Christian community, a fellowship of faith in which shared decision-making is "for real."

First, if you're the pastor, don't miss an opportunity to quote the parish council or refer to it in the pulpit and in the bulletin. It's not enough to publish the minutes. On crucial decisions affecting the whole parish, announce the total vote of the council.

Second, don't miss an opportunity to give visibility to the members of the parish council. After you have presented the theology of liturgical changes, the chairperson of your liturgy committee could announce practical details about the handshake of peace, selection of hymns, and missalettes. If your parish needs lay men and women to distribute Holy Communion, your liturgy committee could be given first consideration. Further, the liturgy committee could announce the practical details for confirmation and offer some visible service in that parish celebration. They could also arrange for an open forum on the renovation of the church or the reasons for First Communion before the sacrament of reconciliation.

Also, the chairperson of your family life committee could announce next Tuesday's anti-abortion meeting or next Sunday's Pre-Cana or Cana Conferences, or married couples retreats.

The chairperson of your administration committee could take the pulpit once a year for a money or budget talk. He/she could also sign the financial reports and financial campaign letters which go out to parishioners.

The chairperson of your education committee, by letter or

by parish meeting, could announce school decisions, such as an increase in tuition, the elimination of uniforms, or bus routes, for the coming school year.

The chairperson of your Christian service committee could announce the names of sick parishioners in the hospital or convalescent home. He/she could also take charge of the Catholic Charities collections.

The chairperson of your ecumenism committee could represent the parish at interfaith prayer meetings and luncheons. Other members of the council could represent the parish at Kiwanis, Rotary or United Way meetings. Such meetings could be reported in the parish paper or council newsletter. There is almost no limit to the opportunities for upgrading the image of the parish council. Then the parishioners will gradually become more interested in the activities of the parish council.

Stimulating Parish Involvement

 How do you get the rest of the parish interested in the work of the parish council?

 This problem is closely related to communication. Apathy may be the result of poor communication.

Some parish councils have generated interest by conducting surveys of all the parishioners on particular problems. Since it causes discussion, a questionnaire is one way of confronting the people with their common problems. This means an investment of time and research, but the tabulated results of such a poll will usually be read with interest.

A parish council needs to have a serious program to win the support and enthusiasm of the people. It needs to provide a true Christian witness to the Gospel in our time and to be responsive to the "signs of the times." Abortion, education, politics, poverty, race, ecumenism—these are only a few of the problems which demand a Christian response. These issues present a real challenge and could deliver the council from its narrow parochialism.

Some councils have taken a census of special talents and interests in the parish. Such a file can be a great help in recruiting more people for *ad hoc* committees. In this way, more of your parishioners can be enlisted in the work of your council because of the unique services which they can bring to the mission of the parish. Enlisting their help may stimulate a greater interest.

No doubt, some people will never become interested. This may be very discouraging for council members, but it is a challenge the true disciple is prepared to accept.

Elections During Mass

Q *Our diocesan guidelines recommend that elections take place at Sunday Mass, with presentation of candidates and their qualifications. I feel the Holy Sacrifice of the Mass should not be interrupted. It deserves the complete and uncluttered attention of the people.*

A We have "interrupted" the Holy Sacrifice of the Mass for many years with ordinations, marriages, funerals, baptisms, confirmations, graduations and *collections*. Such "interruptions" are more correctly viewed as part of the total liturgy which celebrates God's presence in human events.

The liturgy, after all, celebrates God's mighty deeds, not as if they were "up in the sky," but as they are revealed in the actual lives, the flesh and blood, of the believing people.

The process of prayerful discernment, whereby a Christian community selects the leaders who will minister on the council, is indeed a spiritual event. It's at least as spiritual as taking up the collection, an event for which the liturgy is regularly "interrupted." Therefore, I see no reason why elections cannot take place in connection with the Sunday liturgy.

No doubt, such a practice is open to abuse if done poorly. Also, some parishioners may feel it is a profane, "political" intrusion upon their version of the sacred. However, elections can be a teaching moment. A careful preparation and explanation of the spiritual nature of discernment would prevent most of the "scandal" and misunderstanding. Assuming that most pastors would organize elections with a pastoral sensitivity for good liturgy, I would support your diocesan guidelines.

Parish Voter Apathy

 Our problem is apathy. Out of a parish of 900 registered families, we received only 117 votes during a recent election.

Do you have any suggestions for increasing parish participation in elections?

A Apathy will be with us until the coming of the kingdom. The larger the parish, the greater the apathy. However, your small voter turnout may indicate that most of the parish either has never related to the council or has "tuned it out."

After the next election ask each council member to phone ten people on the parish list. Ask these people why they didn't vote. At the following council meeting, let each member report the results of his/her telephone survey. This election feed-back may indicate the steps you need to take to deal with apathy.

In the meantime, here are some suggestions. First, publish your agenda in the Sunday bulletin two weeks before each meeting. Then have each council member call ten parishioners to ask: "Did you see the council agenda in the last Sunday's bulletin?" or "How do you feel about the proposal to cancel the twelve o'clock Mass?" After getting reactions to specific items on the agenda, ask: "Are there any other items you would like to see on future agendas?" If you call ten different names for each meeting, you can go through the whole parish list rather quickly.

Second, publish the highlights of each council meeting in the Sunday bulletin. Be sure the names and phone numbers of council officers are always in the bulletin, so that the people can call them for more information about council decisions.

Third, conduct an open forum twice a year to hear the concerns of the parishioners on topics of broad interest, such as closing the school, the quality of CCD programs, or liturgical changes.

Fourth, make sure the council gets visibility, both in the parish and in the community. Have council committee chairpersons make occasional pulpit announcements on such topics as right to life, finances, or education.

Fifth, send out a council newsletter with your quarterly financial report. The newsletter can carry brief interviews with council members or selected quotes from recent meetings.

Sixth, at election time, introduce all the candidates at all the Sunday Masses. Then encourage parishioners to talk to the candidates over coffee and donuts.

Seventh, make sure that the people know that the council has real, not token, responsibility. The people just will not get involved if the council is viewed as a "rubber stamp."

Eighth, make sure you rotate the membership of the council. If the same people keep running for elections, the council will be viewed as a clique, even if it isn't. The members will be seen as seeking power and status for themselves. That turns everybody off.

Finally, don't get on the telephone after your meetings to tell your friends how awful the meeting was. If you do, you can hardly expect them to jump with ecstatic enthusiasm when you invite them to run for the council when your term is up.

Restricting the Parish Vote

Q *We were getting such a low voter turnout (7%) during our annual election that our council decided to limit the vote to the council's committees. The councillors felt the parishioners didn't know the candidates well enough to cast an intelligent vote. We have a very mobile parish.*

Some of us are very upset by the council's decision. What do you think?

A I can't agree with your council's decision.

Your council is on its way to becoming a clique. It's losing its connection with the rest of the parishioners. It's not holding itself accountable. It's not using the parishioners' discernment gifts in selecting its leaders.

It would be much better to find out *why* you have such a low voter turnout. Is your council already perceived to be a clique? Do you engage the interest of the rest of the parish by publishing the agenda and the highlights of the minutes in the parish bulletin? Do the parishioners have plenty of opportunity to vote? Are your meetings open to the parishioners?

It's true that in some of our highly mobile parishes, the people often do not know the candidates. That's the great challenge for the election committee. To meet that challenge, the committee could set aside at least three months to prepare the people for elections. It could hold coffee and donut receptions to help the parishioners get to know the candidates. It could introduce candidates at all the Sunday Masses and ask them to explain their reasons for running for the council. It could publish an insert for the bulletin with pictures, brief resumes, and other pertinent material.

You will never get a hundred percent voter turnout, but I'm sure you'll do better than seven percent. At any rate, taking the vote away from the people is not the answer.

Improving Parish-Wide Communications

 We have a real problem establishing good communications between the council and the rest of the parish. Any suggestions?

A I won't pretend to have the final answer to this one, but here are some thoughts that might help:

Some parish councils publish a monthly newsletter. Other councils "take over" a page of the parish bulletin after each meeting. Some councils invite an especially competent parishioner to present a paper on a "hot issue" on the agenda. Excerpts are then published in the bulletin.

In one parish, the chairman of the administration commission takes over the pulpit once a year to present a financial report to the people. The chairman of the board of education takes the pulpit for his report at the beginning of the school year.

These are only one-way communications. If people do not read or listen, they still won't know you exist. In large parishes, this is often the case.

THE PASTOR

Pastor's Right to Vote

Q *Our diocesan guidelines do not allow the pastor to vote. How do you feel about this?*

A I don't like it.

The pastor is a baptized Christian. He should be able to vote his Christian opinion just like all the other members of the council. He shouldn't lose his franchise just because he's the pastor.

If the pastor doesn't have a vote, it looks as if the council is set up as a body against him, or at least outside of him. If the council is to be a Christian community of shared responsibility, the pastor should be a full member with equal voting rights.

Besides, councils should not make such a big fuss over the veto power. The pastor may not have to veto anything for ten years. Why should he be deprived of the right to vote during all those years?

Also, the pastor should not have to carry the burden of the veto all by himself. All councillors should assume some responsibility for retaining doctrinal unity with the diocesan and universal church. That's what shared responsibility is all about.

When the pastor vetoes a recommendation, he does so as delegate of the diocesan church. (In the absence of a pastor, the bishop could, of course, delegate a lay administrator to represent the diocesan church and so to exercise a veto.) Since the veto is really a function of the diocesan church, it should remain a separate and distinct act. It should not hover, as an ugly shadow, over the regular voting process.

One final point—it hardly needs saying that the pastor doesn't always agree with diocesan policy. He should, therefore, be able to go on record by voting his disagreement, just like everybody else. Such unanimous disagreement could be communicated to the proper diocesan department to encourage a review of policies.

Reasons for a Veto

Q *Every now and then our pastor vetoes our recommendation. But he never gives us any reasons for the veto. Shouldn't he be required to give his reasons?*

A Yes.
Many council constitutions require the pastor to give his reasons for a veto in writing.

Assuming the pastor is present for council meetings and contributes to the discussion, a veto should be rare. If it does occur, the council may, by two-thirds vote, decide to override it and appeal to the appropriate diocesan office or to the bishop. But the decision to override makes no sense without a thorough discussion of the pastor's reasons for the veto.

By the way, the word "veto" carries a lot of emotional and political baggage. When you revise your constitution, you might substitute the word "ratify." It's more positive and far more descriptive of what actually takes place.

Pastor-Appointed Nominating Committee

Q *In our election only the pastor and two of his old friends make up the nominating committee. So only the pastor's old cronies get on the ballot. The pastor says he knows who is competent and who isn't. But we have a lot of new families in a rather large city parish and they don't know the candidates. Only 250 people bother to vote. The council is only an extension of the pastor's own ideas. The rest of the parish couldn't care less. What should we do?*

A I think you should start all over. Your election was "rigged" right from the start. Evidently, your pastor didn't have enough trust in his people to risk an open election. Afraid of losing control, he manipulated the whole election process.

I doubt whether your council will ever be effective. It's not truly representative. With such a narrow base of support, the parish at large will either oppose or ignore the council.

Your first step in starting over might be a thorough self-evaluation of your present council and its relations with the rest of the parish. An objective inventory of your mistakes is part of the educational process. This may be a bit painful for the pastor and his "cronies," but the problem can't be by-passed.

Second, insist on some kind of educational program for the whole parish before you conduct any election. You might start with a steering committee. Twenty-Third Publications publishes some fine material for this purpose.

Your steering committee could become a laboratory in which the pastor would learn how to relate to a parish council, how to venture out of the protective insulation of his own clique. This period of formation could include small group liturgies, a study of *The Constitution on the Church* and *The Decree on the Laity,* and, finally, the development of communication skills. Gradually, the pastor will learn to trust all his people and to be more receptive to conflicting opinions. He will then be less threatened by an open election.

Pop-In, Pop-Out Pastor

Q   *Our pastor rarely attends a complete meeting of our council. He pops in and out. We have to go over the whole discussion again just for his benefit. This is very time-consuming. Besides, it irks the rest of us. We're just as busy as he is. Any suggestions?*

A   So many unknown factors may be involved here, that it's risky to make suggestions from a distance. The pastor may feel his presence inhibits free discussion. Or, he may really have an extremely busy evening on that particular day of the week. With the present shortage of priests, the parish may be understaffed.

However, I would suggest that you discuss this matter openly and honestly at your earliest opportunity. The chairperson could set the stage for this by regularly allocating some time to critique the meetings. He/she could list this on the agenda as "team evaluation." This is a recommended practice even when everything is going smoothly. During this critique, you or the chairperson could lead off with a candid admission of your own failures, your own neglect of team effort. Your example of openness may move the pastor to admit his own failure to the parish team.

If this doesn't work, just say honestly that you are distressed by the absence of the pastor, that you are hurt by his unfair imposition on your time.

At first, this kind of confrontation may be a bit painful both for you and for the pastor. However, in the long run it's better to say it openly than to complain behind the pastor's back. This kind of direct feedback will foster honesty. It will improve communications for future meetings. It will certainly improve the efficiency of the council.

Pastor as Chairman

Q *Our pastor insists on being chairman of our council meetings. This makes it difficult to question any parish policies. The pastor always gets so defensive. Some members are afraid to express their feelings so directly to the pastor. Others resent the paternalism implied, as if no one else could be a good chairman. What should we do?*

A Chairmanship is a function which is servant to the process and dynamics of the council meeting. It is a skill and art. In the context of a Christian community, it can be charism.

In electing a chairperson, the council recognizes the gift of leadership. Whether this leader turns out to be a priest, a layperson, or a sister, surely isn't important. The council deserves the person who will do the best job.

Neither theology nor the Roman collar guarantees leadership skill in meetings. Nor does our democratic culture look kindly on people who are always "pulling rank." Leadership positions have to be earned. Besides, no one owns the church. Everyone serves it. All are co-workers with God. The church is not divided up into clerics who manage and laity who serve.

In your particular case, you might try an honest dialogue with your pastor in a more private meeting. This may give him a new insight into the human chemistry of the council meeting. If this doesn't work, find out how the other councils in your diocese select their chairperson. If your pastor still insists on appointing himself chairman, check your diocesan guidelines or by-laws.

Theological Knowledge in Policy Decisions

Q *Parish councils do not have the training or theological knowledge to make major policy decisions. They can assist the clergy, but basic policy decisions should be made by the pastor.*

He's the only one on the council who has the proper qualifications of education and experience to make policy decisions.

A You have put your finger on a very real problem. It's true that large numbers of laity have neither the training nor the knowledge to make policy decisions. All across the country, pastors are discovering that the laity elected to the council often know very little about liturgy, religious education, Christian service, and social justice.

No doubt there will always be a knowledge gap between the pastor and the laity. The doctor knows more about medicine than his patients. The lawyer knows more about law than his clients. The pilot knows more about flying than his passengers. Therefore, the pastor knows more about "pastoring" than the laity. After all, he has received four years of special, and rather expensive, graduate education in the seminary. He has had many years of on-the-job training as an associate pastor.

On the other hand, one can hardly exclude the laity from policy decisions merely on the basis of an actual knowledge gap between pastor and laity. After all, the baptized laity do share in the mission of Christ. They possess gifts given by the Spirit according to "the measure of faith," not according to the measure of knowledge. They share responsibility for the proclamation of the Gospel, and such responsibility is meaningless without some real participation in policy decisions.

The knowledge gap, however, remains a serious problem. It just won't do to say: "Laypersons don't need any knowledge; all they need is faith." I'm pleased if my doctor has faith but, if he's going to operate on my ruptured disc, I hope he also has knowledge.

There are at least three different ways in which the parish can deal with the council's lack of training and preparation. First, the election committee can ask that candidates for election commit themselves to attending a weekend workshop or its equivalent as preparation for serving on the council.

Second, the pastor can personally invite councillors to attend adult education courses in liturgy, Scripture, and the church. The finance committee could be asked to budget for the council's education.

Third, the diocese could set up pastoral institutes on a regional basis to train laity for ministry on councils. In an article in *Chicago Studies,* Bishop John Sullivan makes a strong plea for the establishment of such institutes:

> In terms of enlightenment we must start out with a pastoral institute, an institute to equip people for ministry. We could begin with one or two, with a rotating program to prepare people for ministry. I do not know what the curriculum would be but certainly it would include Scripture, religious education, counseling, a variety of programs. That just has to come. Fifteen years ago there were nearly 500 seminaries in this country, religious, diocesan, minor, major; there were seventy-five in one state alone. If we could afford to maintain 500 seminaries, certainly we could start with one or two institutes where we would have a concentration of people in the best of these fields who could reproduce themselves, who could really equip people to minister. We are often presumptuous and we procrastinate. Procrastination and half measures are one of the great problems.

I hope more dioceses will follow Bishop Sullivan's suggestion. It's an idea whose time has come.

Autonomous Pastor

 What use are parish councils? After all kinds of discussion, the pastor does what he wants anyway.

Parish councils aren't any use if the pastor ignores them. If he does, they may even cause bitterness and frustration. They may also turn off the very parishioners who have many gifts and talents to build up the Church.

If your council is merely going through empty motions, if it's not at least trying to be an organism of shared responsibility, you might as well adjourn until a new pastor arrives. There are many other ways in which you can share in the mission of Christ.

On the other hand, don't give up too quickly. Shared ministry won't happen overnight. In some cases, it will be attained only through a painful struggle, lasting for several years. Building a church building is easy; building a real Christian community is tough.

You might take some practical steps in building a Christian community "around" the pastor. He is, after all, a responsive human being who is susceptible to change. He may find it hard to resist the human and divine dynamism of a real faith community.

You might, for starters, devote more of your meeting time to shared prayer and shared reflection on the Scriptures. Your pastor could hardly say "no" to prayer.

Next, try a pizza-and-beer meeting at the chairperson's home or in the pastor's backyard. Such informal sharing may go a long way toward building a trusting and sharing community. Once you have achieved that, it will be a little easier to move into the shared ministry of a parish council.

Once you get to know the pastor, you may discover he isn't really doing "what he wants," but what he sincerely feels he *has to do*. He does, in fact, have to obey the 2,414 church laws, called canons. Then, too, there may be a rather long list of diocesan laws and policies. Besides that, your pastor has to be obedient to church doctrine and the many pastoral regulations covering the celebration of the liturgy and the sacraments.

As you get to know your pastor better, you may decide that he really needs to continue his education in the theory and practice of parish councils. You might ask your diocese to sponsor a parish council workshop or conference for priests. If you offer your support and encouragement, your pastor may be quite willing to attend.

Although you may not get to first base with any of my suggestions, it won't hurt to try. If it doesn't work, offer your gifts to some other Christian apostolate.

Overriding the Pastor

Q *We have a new Director of Religious Education. She relates well to parishioners, but our pastor says she doesn't follow his policies. Therefore, he wants to fire her. Can the parish council veto him?*

A No.
For those who like a simple answer, there it is. A simple monosyllabic "no."

Of course, simple answers often don't deal with the total issue. In this case, for instance, the issue involves the role of the pastor, the policy of the diocese, and the relationship between the pastor and the council. And that covers only the "church" side of the issue. It says nothing about the human and the emotional sides, the rights of employees, or their professional competence.

This time, let's confine ourselves to the church's side of the problem. As we all know, the pastor of a parish wears many hats. He's the official presider over the eucharistic celebration. He's the chief preacher of the Word of God. He shares the bishop's threefold office of *teaching,* ruling, and sanctifying.

Canon law makes him the chief catechist, even though he may be a disaster in the classroom. He is responsible, by virtue of the pastor's office, for overseeing the teaching of Christian doctrine, even though he is a poor teacher.

In the Roman Catholic Church, the pastor is also the manager or administrator of the parish's temporal affairs. That means he's responsible for recruiting, hiring, and firing employees. He also has to sign their contracts and oversee their work. In most cases, he signs their checks. All of this is part of his day-to-day ministry, the ministry of administration. It may not be an ideal system, but that's the way it is.

In many dioceses, the office of education has established policies regarding Religious Education Directors. Pastors are expected to follow recommended norms in setting up their religious education programs.

Also, in many dioceses, the parish council can, by two-thirds majority, appeal a decision of the pastor to the appropriate diocesan office. Sometimes it's the bishop; other times, it's an office for parish councils or parish affairs. Such an appeal doesn't mean that the council vetoes the pastor. It just means that the council is asking for an outside opinion regarding the pastor's decision. That opinion can go either way.

From this distance, I have no idea of how your pastor and your council relate to each other, but I suspect it's not a healthy, trusting relationship.

I suggest you set up an *ad hoc* committee to study all the facts on both sides of the issue. Choose people who have no heavy emotional investment on either side. They could first talk and *listen* to the pastor, to concerned parents, and to the diocesan office. Then they could make a recommendation. In the meantime, your council could carry on with the regular work of the parish without being spiritually and emotionally drained by one issue.

After the *ad hoc* committee has completed its task, the whole council could devote an evening to discernment and prayerful reflection. The *Guidelines* for the Diocese of Columbus recommend: "the council and the entire parish should be called upon to pray intensely for the grace of discernment. A discipline of preparation should characterize the initial stage. Time for quiet, fasting, Scripture reading, setting aside personal ambitions and concerns, Sacrament of Penance, and active listening to the truth of the Lord should be incorporated into parish life and the council's life." I'm sure such an evening will produce a more understanding climate. It could even lead to a solution.

Pastor Rejects the Budget

Q   Our parish council worked hard on a budget for a whole year. Then we got a new pastor. He says he has his own projects and money needs and won't abide by the budget. What should we do?

A   In most cases, the finance committee prepares the budget. The full council, after reviewing and amending it, approves it. Then the committees and full-time staff, including the pastor, operate within that budget. Often councils allow the pastor a discretionary fund to cover emergencies. If committees or full-time staff exceed their budget, they are expected to get approval from the council through the finance committee.

In your case, I would suggest you place the budget on "hold" for awhile. Get the council together for a whole day for a goal-setting workshop. During a brainstorm session, let everybody explain his/her projects. This system will make it easier for the pastor to present his own projects and money needs. Once his projects are out on the table, the council may find them quite acceptable. Then, too, his projects will have to be considered along with everybody else's projects.

It will soon be evident that there isn't enough money for everybody's projects. All council members, including the pastor, will then have to modify their projects or, at least, accept an order of priority in implementing them. The budget can then be determined according to a consensus on the priority of the various projects.

Don't forget to review your own by-laws and constitution to see what they say about the budget. Also, check out the diocesan guidelines, if you have any. Often it's easier to lean on an outside document to solve an internal problem. The discussion becomes less personal and, therefore, less emotional.

Preparing the Pastor

Q *Is the effort to have a council worth it if the pastor is not first prepared and helped to grow into a new leadership style? Isn't it counter-productive to get people's hopes up and then dash them?*

A If the pastor is really *unwilling* to develop a new leadership style, the formation of a council could indeed dash people's hopes. In that case, it might be better to wait for a new pastor.

On the other hand, the very nature of the Christian community as a partnership requires some kind of movement toward *shared* responsibility in the form of the Christian apostolate. We need to move toward the ideal even though, because of human fraility, we falter and stumble along the way.

You might, through your priests' senate, ask the diocese to sponsor continuing education programs for your priests. It's true that, in many dioceses, councils were mandated without much consideration for helping priests to develop a collegial pastoral style. Some pastors went through the motions, but their hearts were not in it.

However, it's quite possible to begin over. The church, Vatican II tells us, is called "to that continuing reformation of which she always has need, insofar as she is an institution of men here on earth."

I'm convinced that most pastors can be re-trained and retooled. They need professionally designed programs which deal with the whole person. They need motivation and support. They need faith in their own capacity to change and grow as pastoral leaders.

One of the more hopeful signs in the church today is the fact that more and more dioceses are now giving the continuing education of clergy the priority it deserves.

Transition Between Pastors

Q *We are revising our parish council constitution. Our pastor wants to insert the following: "when the pastor dies or is transferred, the parish council ceases to exist." Do you think we should insert such a provision in our constitution?*

A No.
It's understandable, however, that a particular pastor might be in favor of such a statement. In the first place, the official Roman documents which give the experimental norms for *diocesan* consultative bodies do, in fact, contain such a provision. Thus, *Ecclesiae Sanctae* (1966) says: "When the see (diocese) falls vacant, the council (senate) of priests ceases to exist ..." A circular letter (1973) from the Sacred Congregation for the Clergy says: "When the See is vacant, the (Diocesan) Pastoral Council ceases."

In the second place, if a parish council is understood as *merely advisory to the pastor,* it really has nothing to do when the pastor is dead. It has no reason to exist.

Regarding the "norms" of the Roman documents, it's quite clear from the introduction that they were published on an "experimental basis only." While the code of canon law is in a long process of revision, the "norms" don't have the force of law. Even if they did, they would have to be interpreted narrowly. They could not be extended to include parish councils for which they were never intended.

Naturally, I do not believe parish councils are *merely* advisory. And, of course, they do not belong to the pastor. They belong to the Christian community, the local church. All parish structures (buildings, such as churches and schools, and people structures, such as councils and organizations) belong to the community called "parish." The pastor, like the council itself, ministers within that church. He is not the owner; he is one of the many servants passing through the parish.

While the pastor's office is vacant, the council could carry on with the work of the *Lord,* overseeing the programs which have already been approved. Naturally, it should not make any major *new* decisions until the new pastor arrives. *Legally,* it doesn't have any more authority than the temporary administrator who "holds" the parish until a new pastor is appointed.

This question does, however, point out the tension which presently exists between a legal or juridical approach to the Christian apostolate and a more biblical or baptismal view.

In the juridical approach, lay persons, in spite of their baptism, first need authorization to assume their place in the apostolate of the hierarchy. They need a specific mandate, a "canonical" mission, from a bishop or cleric. In this view, lay persons and councils are primarily the aides and instruments of the pastor. They are delegated or "charged" by the pastor or bishop. Such delegation can be given, then taken away, by a decision of the pastor. This approach is not always free from a certain arbitrariness and paternalism.

This juridical view is held by many in the church today. It evokes the image of the pyramid. In this structure, full authority resides at the top, then flows, through law or delegation, to the various "levels" below. It's a view which emphasizes law and jurisdiction as a means of achieving order in the church. In a pluralist church, there is room for such an approach.

Vatican II, however, clearly teaches that the people of God participate in the apostolate of the church by virtue of their Baptism and Confirmation: "... all are commissioned to that apostolate by the Lord himself." (*Constitution on the Church*). They don't need a special mandate or permission from the clergy to share in the apostolate of the church. Their official call comes from the Lord. First given at Baptism, it is renewed at every eucharistic celebration.

Naturally, the baptized need to minister in the *common* apostolate in an order of relationships. They need to relate their ministries to all the other ministries in the church, including those of the ordained priests. There's no Lone Ranger ministry in the church.

In the biblical or baptismal view, the Christian apostolate does not really "wait on" any one law or person, such as the pastor or the bishop. Should the pastor die, the baptismal commitment continues, as do the responsibility of discipleship, the call to witness to the Gospel, and the Christian vocation.

Above all, the dynamic activity of the Spirit continues. "He distributes special graces among the faithful of every rank. By these gifts, He makes them fit and ready to undertake the various tasks or offices advantageous for the renewal and upbuilding of the church'' (*Constitution on the Church*).

Even, and especially, if the pastor dies, all the baptized are called to continue the priestly, prophetic and kingly mission of Jesus Christ. That's what the parish council is all about. If it isn't, then it should indeed cease to exist.

The church, even at the parish "level," is *God's* mystery. Many different pilgrim servants pass through God's church. With their Spirit-given charisms, they labor in God's vineyard, building God's edifices, cultivating God's field. Neither the building nor the cultivating stops just because one of the "fellow laborers" is called to render an account of his or her stewardship.

Friction with the Pastor

Q   *We have a very poor relationship with our pastor. He will not attend our meetings because he disagrees with us on one issue. We're stymied.*

A   With the help of an outside facilitator, devote a whole meeting to leveling with each other on this issue. Write down the areas of agreement, then the areas of disagreement. Once you have figured out the areas of agreement, you could agree to work together on these issues. Then, after praying together, you might agree to tolerate or *accept* each other in the area of disagreement. Most councils have to work together despite some conflict. It's most important, however, to allow the area of conflict to surface. Once it has surfaced and been accepted, you can even have a sense of humor about it while working together on the large areas of agreement.

Council Voice in New Pastor

Q   *When a pastor dies or is transferred, do you feel the parish council should be consulted about a successor?*

A   Yes.

Many Priests' Personnel Boards already consult parish councils before recommending a particular priest for appointment to a parish. Councils can be a great help in providing a profile of the parish, its special needs, and problems.

On the other hand, councils need to remember that they can't have the last word. The priest is ordained for the *diocese*. The council's desire for a particular priest has to be balanced with the needs of the diocese and the needs and charisms of the priest himself.

Parish councils need to be more realistic. They often ask for Jesus Christ. However, they have to learn to be satisfied with whatever ordained manpower is available, with its human limitations and deficiencies. As the shortage of priests becomes more critical, it will also become more difficult for bishops to find a priest who responds perfectly to a particular parish's needs.

At the same time, councils need to remember that they are not infallible in diagnosing their own needs. Although they may feel they need a priest who is a good builder, they may really need a prophetic priest who pushes them to get off the "building binge." They may *want* a popular personality; they may *need* an angry prophet.

QUALITIES OF COUNCIL MEMBERS

Rubber-Stamp Members

 Most of our councillors were appointed by the pastor. They are all his rubber-stamp people. They don't want to say anything "to upset Father." For the rest of us, the council meetings are a waste of time.

A Appointments to the council should be kept to a minimum —two or three at the most.

In the first place, in our democratic society, the parishioners' vote should be respected. Second, the council should not even *appear* to be the pastor's clique of "yes men" or even *his* advisory body. The council is called to be a Christian community, a microcosm of the parish community. The members get their responsibility for the apostolate of the church directly from baptism, not from appointment by the pastor.

Appointments, if they are necessary, should not be made without clear and more-or-less obvious reasons. Nor should they be made without prior consultation with the full council.

Even though we live in a democracy, we can't rule out appointments entirely. Sometimes a pastor needs to make appointments to fill in the gaps in representation; for example, he may need more women, Indians, Blacks, or Mexicans. Other times he needs to make up for the gaps in competence or function by appointing an educator, a liturgist, or a finance administrator.

If your council is nothing more than the pastor's rubber stamp, it's best to dissolve it and start over.

Non-Contributing Members

 We have two men on our parish council who never contribute anything: everything is always "okay" with them. We could recommend burning the church down and they would go along with it. What can we do to get them interested?

A This sounds like a real challenge for the other council members.

From this distance, I can only speculate about possible reasons for the two men's lack of interest.

I suggest that the chairperson talk to each of these men privately. He or she might try to get at their feelings about the council idea itself. He or she might inquire about their reactions to their own election and discover that everything is not really okay.

They may be afraid to express themselves openly in the presence of the pastor. They may be a bit overwhelmed by the more educated members of the council. Or their opinions may have been slapped down by the chairperson at an earlier meeting; perhaps they can't muster the courage "to get hit again."

It's possible, too, that they simply aren't willing to invest time and energy in such a new idea. By temperament, they may not be disposed to the risks of experiment. They may want to bet on a sure winner. But the two silent men are the only ones who can give you the answer.

In the meantime, different methods of motivation could be tried. The two could be invited to gather "a fact sheet" for a particular item on the next meeting's agenda. If the topic is within their own experience, they will feel comfortable about their project and will feel they can make a unique contribution. Once they have completed some kind of research, however elementary, they could become resource persons for further discussions.

Again, another person on the council could play the role of the two silent men. He could verbalize the feelings of the two men as he knows them from private conversation, and "include" the men in his or her comments. This may bring some hidden conflicts out into the open, but that may be all to the good. If council meetings never generate any conflict, some members are not really saying what they feel. Such councils may be "playing games."

There may be a temptation to ease these silent men out of the council and replace them with "live" members. This could be a mistake. If a council cannot motivate these people to greater participation, I suspect something more serious is wrong with the council itself.

Council Apathy and Absenteeism

 Our parish council is suffering from apathy and lack of interest. We are five years old. We have a continuing problem

with absenteeism and resignations. We need to recapture some of our early enthusiasm. We feel we need some kind of renewal, but we don't know how to go about it.

A You might try *Recycling the Parish* published by the National Council of Catholic Laity, Washington, D.C. It could be just the thing for you.

Recycling the Parish is a workbook which outlines a continuous process for council renewal. It consists of ten chapters, or "Learning Aids," which can be concentrated in one weekend workshop or spread out over the year. The accent is on participation and process rather than on instruction or content. It is meant to be a practical aid in the movement toward shared responsibility.

The first of ten sessions consists of a group liturgy. This is an effort to build a climate of faith and set the tone for all the sessions. The second session is an exercise in goal setting. Factors to be considered in this exercise "are not principally cognitive, but also in the domain of attitudes, values and feelings ... Goals should be clear, realistic and evaluable."

The booklet recognizes that "participatory institutions that work are very difficult to come by." It avoids long haggling over the veto power; it concentrates instead on the dynamics of consensus decision-making. It includes extremely helpful suggestions about the art of being a chairperson, the resolution of conflict, the art of listening, and the physical climate of council meetings.

A section on brainstorming gives the following advice: "1) Be spontaneous: say whatever comes to mind. 2) Be non-judgmental: listen to other ideas and build on them. 3) Nothing is too crazy to be considered. 4) Do not censor ideas. 5) Try for quantity: keep it flowing. 6) Do not discuss any ideas until brainstorming is over."

The seventh session includes some practical principles for adult learning. "Adults are responsible for their own learning ... Adults are righ resources for one another's learning ... In any group of adults there is a variety of motivations, learning needs, and degrees of readiness to learn."

The last chapter is concerned with evaluation. It recognizes that, for many people, evaluation has a negative connotation; it tries to reduce people's fears by accenting the positive aspects of "feedback." It outlines an evaluation procedure known as the "paired interview." But no other evaluative forms are suggested, and this is the weakest part of the booklet. No doubt experts in group dynamics could offer other suggestions in structuring the process of evaluation.

Each chapter contains a rather extensive bibliography. A positive tone is maintained throughout. This in itself should be a welcome sign of "life" for those who think the parish is dying.

Increasing Teamwork

Q *Some of us are anxious to improve the efficiency of our parish council team. Do you have any suggestions?*

A This is largely a question of attitude. Council members need to be disposed to improve the human chemistry of the council. They must be convinced of their great potential for growth.

The council could call a special meeting to address itself to the problem of teamwork. Or again, the chairperson could allocate some time each meeting to critique the team process. Once all members become accustomed to this process, it will gradually become an ongoing function of every meeting.

The Managerial Grid Seminars conducted by Scientific Methods, Incorporated have discovered some common barriers to effective teamwork. These barriers are defects in the following elements: 1) candor; 2) critique (either ongoing or in summary); 3) good communication (primarily a failure to listen); 4) planning and preparation; 5) identification of conflict; 6) utilization of conflict; 7) full team input; 8) data recall; 9) eliciting maximum information available; 10) clear identification of problems; 11) commitment to the team concept; and 12) team responsibility for progress of the meetings.

I would suggest that a list of these barriers to effective teamwork could form the agenda for your self-evaluation. It is true some feelings may be hurt in such an open session, and all members need to be sensitive to this danger. However, no council will grow into a good team without some suffering. In fact, such a death is the key to growth. This is the death the council members suffer for upbuilding of the total parish community.

The Rubber-Stamp Council

Q *In our council, the executive committee decides everything before the meeting. The rest of us are expected to give our okay to its decisions. What should we do about this?*

A Check your constitution and by-laws. What are the powers and responsibilities of your executive committee?

In most cases, the executive committee prepares the agenda. Sometimes it calls for special meetings of the full council. In any case, the executive committee should not have any more power than the full council delegates to it. It serves the council; it doesn't replace it.

I suspect you need to revise your constitution. I suggest you place "the role of the executive committee" on the agenda for your next meeting. You need to clear the air in an open discussion. If your council members are merely acting as a rubber stamp for the executive committee, they will soon lose interest and stop coming to the meetings.

The Chair-Warmers

Q *The chair-warmers bother me the most. They appear at every meeting and contribute nothing. They refuse to serve on any committees. They vote only after they see how the pastor is voting. How do we deal with this problem?*

A Confront them in a Christian manner, privately. Those who serve on the council have to be held accountable for their service or *for their lack of service.*

Also, check your election process. Make sure all nominees are aware that they are expected to serve on council committees. Some councils conduct an orientation session for all candidates before elections to make sure that candidates clearly understand the responsibilities of ministry on the council. Although membership on the council is an honor, it's not merely honorary.

Dealing with Absenteeism

Q *Our problem is the lack of commitment on the part of some council members who rarely attend meetings, yet feel no obligation to resign. We don't know what to do about this.*

A First, you might visit the absentees in their homes and ask them why they miss so many meetings. In the privacy of their own turf, they are more apt to express their real feelings: they may feel the council has no real authority; they may feel hurt; they may have lost interest because they ended up on the wrong committee or on no committee; or they may have a conflict with the date of the meeting. Once you know the real reason, you can deal with the issues behind absenteeism.

Some councils ask for a member's resignation if he/she misses three consecutive meetings without an excuse; others allow only three unexcused absences a year.

When candidates are nominated for the council, they should receive a special orientation. It should clearly explain the expectations and time commitments which go with ministry on the council. If candidates, for whatever reason, can't do the work, they should be advised not to accept nomination.

If an elected member constantly misses meetings, some one has to deliver the message: "Paint or get off the ladder!" Commitment is of the essence; without it, the council might as well dissolve.

Tag-Along Members

Q *In our parish, we have many couples who have made the Marriage Encounter. The husband and wife insist on doing everything together. So when the wife is elected to the council, the husband comes to the meetings too. And he gets to vote like everybody else. Do you think that's right?*

A No.
When the parishioners cast their votes to elect the wife, they don't intend to vote for the husband. Togetherness is okay; but the council has to respect the vote of the people.

Elected members have "earned" the right to vote because they were chosen by their fellow parishioners. It's a mockery of the election process and an insult to the electors to give equal voice to someone who was not elected. The representative principle is not absolute. But in a democratic society it needs to be respected. If, for the sake of togetherness, the husband wants to come to the meeting, that's fine. But he should sit with the visitors.

FINANCES

Controlling Parish Funds

Q   *I feel the parish council should not have any control over the parish funds. The laity just does not know anything about the real needs or the mission of the average parish. For instance, in its annual budget, our council allowed a mere hundred dollars for adult education. The laity on the council said: "Adults don't need any education because they had their catechism lessons in school."*

A   If councils are going to be organs of shared responsibility, they will need to share responsibility for expenditure of funds. Councils will mature only if they are given real, not token, responsibility.

Unfortunately, while councils are in the learning stage, they make decisions out of ignorance. This means that they will make mistakes. However, today's empty church buildings in this country prove that the laity have no monopoly on errors of judgment.

No doubt, many laity serving on councils need more instruction in the mission of the church and the parish. Giving them that instruction is the priest's special responsibility. For this reason, many parishes require councillors to attend a weekend workshop on the needs and mission of the parish.

However, ignorance on the council is merely part of a larger problem—the critical need for continuing education of adults. In many cases, the laity who learned their "once-and-for-all" catechism must be made aware of their need for adult education. Today, there are many instruments available which are professionally designed to bring the laity's needs to surface.

Granted, a hundred dollars isn't much. Still, if you used it all to educate your parish council, you would be off to a flying start. For survey forms and more information about the methods for adult education, write to: Office of Adult Education, 320 Cathedral Street, Baltimore, MD 21201 or Office of Continuing Education, P.O. Box 907, Houston, TX 77001.

Financial Power

Q *Who has the final say on how money is spent in the parishes?*

A Sometimes it's the bishop; sometimes it's the pastor; and sometimes it's the parish council. It depends on the amount of money and the purpose for which it's spent. Most dioceses have an established policy, administered with flexibility.

In some dioceses, the pastor may spend up to ten thousand dollars without getting permission from the bishop. (In other dioceses, the established figure may be considerably less.) If the amount to be spent is below that figure, the pastor has the final say. In actual practice, many pastors share with their councils some responsibility for all large expenditures. Yet they can't give the council the final say if the amount is above the figure established by the diocese.

On the other hand, if the school boiler blows up in the dead of winter, the pastor will probably have it fixed without bothering to call either the bishop or the finance committee. In many parishes, the council budget gives the pastor a discretionary fund to cover emergencies. He can hardly be expected to call a meeting of the finance committee every time the school bus breaks down. This discretionary fund, as part of the annual budget, is submitted to the full council for approval.

The Financial Statement

Q *Our council spends entirely too much time questioning the monthly financial statement. Most of the members don't know how to read it properly, and they quibble and haggle over the smallest items. By the time they approve our report, half the meeting is wasted. How do we deal with this problem?*

A Make sure the members receive the financial report, as well as the agenda well in advance of the meeting, so that they can study it on their own time.

When you prepare your council agenda, note which items are for 1) decision, 2) discussion, and 3) *information*. If your financial report is labeled *information* rather than discussion, members will respond accordingly.

You might introduce your report by reminding the members that the council discusses *policy matters only,* adding that you will be happy to discuss "small items" in your report *after* the meeting. The purpose of the report is mainly to show accountability and to *inform* the full council how the parish stands in relation to its approved budget.

The Finance Committee

Q *I feel the diocese should set a definite limit on the amount of money that the finance committee may spend. I know of one parish where the finance committee took complete financial control, hiring the housekeeper and telling the pastor what food, clothing, and supplies he could buy. The pastor became a virtual prisoner of the finance committee. He finally left the priesthood, but he endured an unbelievable "hell" for several years before leaving.*

A Most dioceses do, in fact, limit the amount of money a *pastor* may spend. The amount varies from diocese to diocese. In Detroit, pastors may spend up to $10,000 without asking for permission from the chancery office.

I would assume that a finance committee would be bound by the same limit as that set for the pastor. No doubt, it would be helpful if the diocesan limit were mentioned in the council's by-laws. That way, the finance committee would be warned not to pass a recommendation whose price tag exceeds the diocesan limit.

Most finance committees manage the regular parish finances through an annual budget. They do not, however, have *final authority* to approve the budget. That decision is the responsibility of the full council.

The annual budget should be a realistic response to a council consensus on parish and diocesan goals and priorities. The full council may need a weekend workshop to achieve consensus on short and long-range goals. Parish programs flow from parish goals, and parish budgets flow from programs. If the finance committees follow this system, the annual budget will contain no surprises.

I don't see how a finance committee could have anything to say about what clothes the pastor buys. Such personal expenses come out of the pastor's salary. Whether the pastor buys his suit from K-Mart or from Hong Kong is his business. The cost of running the rectory is part of the operational expenses and comes under the annual parish budget.

Finance committees often get "high and mighty." Actually, they should have no more authority than the other standing committees. All committees are merely the working arms of the full council. No committee should have authority to set parish policies. Only the full council can do that.

Unfortunately, some parishes have placed all the power in the separate committees. This often creates a many-headed monster in which one committee overlaps or competes with another, as some parish societies used to do. The committees tend to become separate entities, with only a loose connection to the council. With such strong emphasis on the individual committees, the council can't grow into a real Christian community in which shared decisions flow from community prayer and common discernment. The council often falls victim to the pressure tactics of vested interests in which the committee that shouts the loudest gets the most attention and money.

Of course, the full council is responsible for holding the reins on a runaway, power-hungry finance committee. However, if the full council can't do it, the problem should be submitted to diocesan arbitration before the pastor gets ulcers or leaves the priesthood.

Finance Committee Authority

Q *We belong to one of three parishes which got together to hire one regional coordinator of religious education. Each parish pays one third of his salary. Now the members of the finance commission of our parish council do not like this coordinator's new catechetics, so they want to eliminate the $4,000 for his salary from next year's budget. In effect, this means the coordinator would be fired. This caused a heated discussion during our last council meeting. Nothing was settled. What should we do?*

A This seems to be another case where the finance commission has overstepped its authority. Finance commissions don't have the power to hire and fire religion coordinators. They should not have such control over the budget that they can, in effect, determine parish policies. Dismissal of a religion coordinator, because of his "new catechetics," is a policy decision which is the responsibility of the pastor, in consultation with the board of education.

A number of issues are involved here. First, there is the question of "new catechetics." This is a concern for the parents and the whole parish staff. This issue might better be discussed in a wide open meeting with resource persons such as theologians and educators. The finance commission is hardly competent to make a decision about such a complex issue.

Second, this case involves not one, but three parishes. It points out the need for some kind of regional council structure which helps different parish councils to work together on mutual problems and projects. Some parishes are still inclined to be parochial and even competitive. This often leads to arbitrary and unilateral decisions which show no concern for the needs of other parishes. In this particular case, the finance commission is ignoring the other two parishes which deserve to be partners in a consensus decision regarding the religion coordinator.

Third, the religion coordinator has a right to know his accusers and to hear their objections. He also has a right to defend himself and his "new catechetics" in the presence of the education committee. The council, after all, is first a Christian community which encourages openness, brotherhood, dialogue, and hospitality.

Publishing Donor List

Q   *Our parish publishes an annual financial report which gives the names and the total contributions of everybody in the parish. This practice has caused a lot of controversy in the finance commission of our parish council. Most of us are against the practice. Many parishioners hate this "scandal sheet." Many new people refuse to register in the parish. Still, the pastor is determined to publish the names because he wants "to put the heat on the deadbeats." We have not been able to resolve this issue. What should we do?*

A   "Putting the heat on the deadbeats" is an old argument for publishing names and amounts of contributions, but I'm not sure it works. Is it worth alienating so many in the parish just to embarrass a few extra bucks out of the "deadbeats?"

Then, too, one wonders about the propriety of appealing to human respect as a motive for giving to the church. Is it really Christian to encourage the parishioners to judge their neighbors concerning their support of the church? Would it not be better to teach respect for the conscience and freedom of every individual? The church is only one of the many worthy causes which commend themselves to the Christian conscience.

Besides, dollars and cents are no real indication of the actual sacrifice of the individual contributor. In the story about the widow's mite (Mark 12:41-44), Jesus commends the poor widow who put into the temple treasury the equivalent of a penny: "I want you (disciples) to observe that this poor widow contributed more than all the others who donated to the treasury. They gave from their surplus wealth, but she gave from her want all that she had to live on."

Jesus also rebuked the Scribes and Pharisees who gave alms to be seen by men (Matthew 6:1-4). Christians giving alms are not to blow a horn "like hypocrites looking for applause." "In giving alms you are not to let your left hand know what your right hand is doing." Thus, Jesus makes a distinction between the spurious piety of display and genuine piety which seeks to conceal itself.

What should your parish council do? Since the "scandal sheet" appears to be a matter of parish policy, you might, first of all, discuss it at an open meeting of the entire council. Second, you might take a survey of all the parishioners to find out how they feel about "the sheet." Third, you might experiment for a year with an appeal to higher motivation. The totals of your next financial report might convert your pastor.

Overemphasis on Money

 Our parish council continues to spend most of its time on finances. How can we get out of this rut?

A There's no easy solution, but I can share some ideas I picked up at various council meetings. First, insist on a brief reading of an appropriate Scripture passage at the beginning of each meeting. This will set the proper tone.

Second, arrange the printed agenda so finances will be last.

Third, do not read financial reports during the meeting. They should be mailed with the agenda *before* the meeting, so that members can read them on their own time.

Fourth, insist that the finance committee meet separately before the full council meets. Most of the dollars and cents discussion should take place at that committee meeting. The council must trust the committee. The council should ask questions only about implementation of goals and objectives and about broad policy matters.

Parish Maintenance

Q *We are just a glorified maintenance committee. During the last meeting, we spent three hours talking about shower heads, new screens, carpeting, door locks, coat racks, an incinerator and a cement job. These meetings get pretty boring because we never discuss litrugy, education, or any broad parish policies. What should we do?*

A All the items you listed could be quickly settled in a separate meeting of your administration committee. One member of that committee, who serves on the council, could then give a two-minute report to the parish council.

Unfortunately, many parish councils in the beginning stages devote too much time to finance and maintenance problems. This is frequently a reaction to the crisis of the moment. Again, many lay people feel more comfortable and competent in these areas than in the areas of liturgy and education.

If councils spent some time during each meeting reading selections from the Scriptures and discussing the purpose of their parish, council meetings would soon reflect a broader view than the "nuts and bolts" of maintenance.

DIOCESAN CONCERNS

Meeting with the Bishop

 Why can't the bishop meet with our parish council when he comes for confirmations?

A It's quite possible that he can. In many cases, he does. The next time your parish is scheduled for confirmations, why don't you invite him? Get your questions ready, because there's a good chance he'll meet with you.

Diocesan Veto Power

 How come the diocesan consultors can, in a secret meeting, override the decisions of our council?

A Legally, the diocesan church retains veto power over the council in doctrinal, liturgical, and canonical matters. In these three areas, the diocesan consultors, representing the diocesan church and acting *in union with their bishop,* can indeed override a council's decisions. It's a poor example of shared ministry, but it's legal.

However, an earthy instinct tells me your dispute is about money. If so, it's a little harder to defend the power of the diocesan church to override. If your council is rejecting a diocesan assessment, I would have to know the reasons for the disagreement. A difference of opinion regarding parish and diocesan priorities ought to be subject to dialogue, not to secret veto.

More and more dioceses have set up standing arbitration committees. If your diocese has such a committee, your council could ask for a hearing. If it has none, write a letter and ask the bishop to appoint one.

Diocesan Certification

 Our chancery office has decreed that all council constitutions must be certified by the diocese. We disagree. We feel

there can be several good models for a parish council. We don't think the diocese should force one model on every parish.

A Let's try a little positive thinking. Certification could mean that the bishop makes a firm commitment to support your constitution and your council. This would mean that a new pastor could not dissolve your council just because he doesn't like your constitution. Also, he couldn't force you to adopt the constitution he brought along from St. Cunegunda's. In other words, if you get into trouble following a certified constitution, you can rightly look to the diocese for help. (If I were a bishop, I would certainly not support some of the strange constitutions I've seen.)

Certification by the diocese, therefore, can be a positive commitment to the continuity of your council. In this way, laypersons will feel better about investing themselves in your council. They will know that the council won't evaporate into thin air the day the pastor has a fatal heart attack.

Needless to say, certification should be a flexible process, looking more to the spirit than to the letter of the law. It should indeed allow for a certain diversity of council models. On the other hand, it should look for a certain unity with the mission and the priorities of the diocesan church. The diocese can rightly expect a core committee system, such as education, worship, or Christian service. Certification can build a more positive linkage with the diocesan church and so deliver the council from its parochial and congregationalist tendencies. In general, certification, if administered in a flexible and supportive way, can be a real plus for the council. The diocese is not an angry policeman; it's a support system.

Diocesan Authority

 I feel each parish should have authority to decide the kind and number of committees it should have on the council. Our diocese, in its proposed new guidelines, is trying to impose a set committee system for every parish. It's another example of the diocesan bureaucracy trying to tell all the parishes what to do. I think each parish should be allowed to develop its own model.

A I can't agree.
The parish is a cell within the body that is the diocesan

church. As the hand and the feet are in continuity with the body, each parish needs to be in continuity with the pastoral mission of the diocesan church.

Continuity doesn't mean a rigid, militaristic uniformity. Parishes need to retain some flexibility to respond to local needs. A Mexican or Black parish won't be organized on the same patterns as a White parish in the suburbs.

On the other hand, it seems to me the diocesan church could insist on a core committee system, with the local options to add other committees and to adapt the form of the core committees. Thus, a diocese could, for the sake of diocesan unity, ask that every council have committees on education, liturgy and service. Without these three functions, the parish could hardly be seen as a cell in the body that is the diocesan church.

Regional Cooperation

Q *Our diocese, which is rather large, has recently been divided into six regions. However, our diocesan council guidelines totally ignore the new regions. Why can't councils be organized on a regional basis?*

A I'm very much in favor of regional cooperation between parish councils. Often in the same diocese, one region's needs and resources are entirely different from those of another. Then, too, many city-wide problems are too big for one parish to tackle alone. And more importantly, such inter-council cooperation delivers the parish from narrow parochialism. If regional councils are united in one bread and one cup, they should also be united in one mission.

However, I'm not sure such inter-council cooperation needs to be structured "from above" by diocesan guidelines. I see no reason why the councils of a region couldn't simply agree to work together on local issues. They could meet together, say twice a year. They could exchange agendas and minutes. They could avoid competitive and overlapping programs and work together on the common issues.

On the other hand, we shouldn't build our expectations too high. Salvation is not regionalization.

Dividing dioceses into smaller regions is an effort to make the large dioceses more manageable. It looks great on paper. It can even be promoted by high-sounding rhetoric about subsidiarity. But I doubt if it will really work in the long run. It side-steps the larger and more important questions. Why is the diocese so large in the first place? Why not create a new diocese?

Vatican II's *Decree on the Pastoral Office of Bishops* recommended as one option that dioceses be divided: "therefore, as regards diocesan boundaries, the sacred Synod decrees that insofar as the good of souls requires it, a prudent revision of diocesan boundaries be undertaken as soon as possible. This can be done by dividing, distributing, or uniting dioceses, changing their boundaries, or appointing a more suitable place for the episcopal see ..."

Pope Paul VI's, *Ecclesiae Sanctae* (1966) containing the norms for the implementation of the *decree* on bishops, asks national episcopal conferences to set up a special study commission "to secure the proper revision of the boundaries of dioceses." It even recommends "that the assistance of laymen ... be invited." In England, such a commission recommended that the number of dioceses be doubled.

Experiments with regionalization have produced mixed results. A region has no distinct eucharistic base. It doesn't gather as a community on the day of the Lord to celebrate the Eucharist. The regional apostolate doesn't flow from a regional liturgy.

There are many canon laws to cover the operation of parishes and dioceses. There are none for the region. All serious regional decisions have to wait for approval by the bishop. No one pastor really has enough authority to decide the issue and move the region to action. In the crunch, most priests still look to the bishop, not to the regional dean, for the final word.

Since regions often can't deal with the larger issues, they waste a lot of time on "pious piffle." Too many meetings which "don't go anywhere" build up considerable frustration.

For these reasons, regional organization will achieve very limited objectives. In most cases, councils would do well to devote at least some of their energies to push for the creation of a new diocese.

AREAS OF CONFLICT

Conflict Between Committees

Q *I am a member of our parish board of education. Our board is one of the five commissions which make up our parish council. We have a problem with the parish council, especially with the members of the finance commission. They always want to cut our budget. They want to save more money for CCD, adult education, and other groups. Yet we can't run a school without sufficient funds. How do we settle this argument?*

A This controversy, in one form or another, comes up at many council meetings. I'm not sure anyone can "settle" it.

One thing is certain: if a parish council has made a policy decision to keep the school open, it will have to provide adequate funds. Quality education costs money. Finance commissions are frequently at fault here. They often assume the policy-making role which belongs only to the full council. Like the other commissions, including the board of education, the finance commissions are *functional*. They carry out policies. They do not determine them.

However, this controversy has deeper roots. It's basically a disagreement about priorities in the mission of the parish. Parish councils are unfairly blamed for questioning the growing financial outlay for schools. Yet councils would be useless if they did not seriously evaluate the mission of the parish in view of the changing needs of the church and the world. The teaching function of the church, through schools, is only one of many other functions in the broader mission of the church.

In addition to its teaching (prophetic) function, the church also has sanctifying (priestly) and ruling (kingly) functions. Thus, the teaching mission is not absolute, but relative.

In the teaching mission of the church, Vatican II, like the New Testament, distinguishes between two forms: one is called *kerygma;* the other is called *didascalia*. The first is the missionary proclamation of the Good News to the non-baptized; the second is the authorized teaching of doctrine to the baptized.

The first is exemplified by the Gospel of Mark: "The time is fulfilled, and the kingdom of God is at hand; repent and believe in the Gospel ... He is risen ... Go preach the Gospel to the whole creation." The second is found in parts of Luke and St. Paul's pastoral letters. In the struggle with the Gnostic heresy, Paul warned his Christians at Ephesus: "... guard the truth which has been entrusted to you ... follow the pattern of sound words which you have heard from me." This teaching is defensive; its purpose is to *establish* believers in the faith.

Vatican II recovered a truth of the early church when it declared that the missionary proclamation to non-Christians is primary and the teaching of doctrine to Christians is secondary. (To say that it's secondary doesn't mean it's unimportant.)

In light of this, parish councils need to ask questions about their own priorities. How much money is budgeted for the sanctifying function of the church (for liturgy, prayer, reconciliation, and other functions)? Then, how much money is budgeted for the parish's missionary proclamation, in word and deed, in its own area and in the world? To what extent does the parish witness, in time and money, to its *Catholic* name in preaching the Gospel to the poor at home and abroad?

Next, how much money is budgeted for the secondary form of teaching, establishing the baptized believer in sound doctrine? This budget can further be sub-divided into a twofold order of priority: first, according to teaching methods, such as television, radio, newspaper, home visitation, CCD, and school; second, according to special groups, such as adults, children, college students, priests, teachers, and senior citizens. Each group has different needs at different times.

Determination of budget is not simply a response to the demands of an existing building; it is an evaluation of the mission of the church and the "signs of the times."

It may mean eliminating some classrooms or even closing the school. However, such policy-decisions are not the responsibility of the finance commission or the board of education, but of the whole parish council.

Avoiding Factionalism

 Our council is composed primarily of the representatives of our parish organizations who are interested only in the ac-

tivities of their organizations. (The Men's Club is sponsoring a dance. The Altar Society has a bake sale.) They just don't know what a council should be. How do we get these people interested in the larger goals of the parish?

A Your best bet is to start over. Add some new parishioners to your present council and convert it into a steering committee. Then you'll be ready to begin a twelve month educational program.

You have to educate your own committee first. You can buy all kinds of fine resource materials from Twenty-Third Publications. With study materials in hand, you'll be ready to meet and discuss what a parish council should be and do.

After everybody on your committee has a clear understanding of the purpose of a council, you'll be ready to begin an educational program for your parish and its organizations.

In no case should parish organizations *dominate* the council. If the parish organizations are truly apostolic, and not merely social, they should serve on the council's committees. But the council itself should not become top-heavy with numerous representatives from the parish organizations. The council has work to do. It should not use up all its energies trying to represent absolutely everybody.

Divisive Factions

Q *Our parish council is divided into two factions: those who want to keep the old ways and those who want change and experimentation. We can't agree on anything and spend most of our time arguing. What should we do about our council?*

A The bishops of Vatican II were also divided into two factions: those who wanted change and those who wanted to stand pat. Nevertheless, through prayer, study, dialogue, and the help of the Spirit, they managed to achieve a consensus on sixteen documents covering the main problems of the church.

Since the First Council of Jerusalem, when the Gentiles were given equal status with Jewish Christians, we have always lived in a pluralist church. We've had Eastern and Western versions of Christianity. We've lived with Franciscan, Dominican, and Jesuit theologies. We've worked with monarchic, hierarchic, and democratic models of church.

Since parish councils represent the church, they also reflect the church's pluralism. This means that a broad spectrum of "theological" opinion may be present in every council meeting. Sometimes this spectrum is simplistically reduced to two factions: liberal and conservative. This isn't all bad. Two different points of view can generate a lively dialogue. A dialectical tension can clarify old ideas and give birth to new ones. Conflict can be utilized creatively.

The best way to deal with factions on the council is to go away on a weekend workshop. Invite an outside facilitator who has special expertise in group dynamics and conflict resolution to conduct the workshop.

You can start the workshop by listing the broad areas in which you are definitely united: one Christ, one Gospel, one baptism, one cup, one bread, one church, and so forth. You will be amazed to discover how many areas of agreement you actually have. Then everyone on the council will know that it's really not true to say: "We can't agree on anything."

After defining the areas of agreement, list the areas of disagreement. Be careful not to allow any moralistic judgments to be made. Council members do not become good or bad for holding a specific opinion or for belonging to one faction rather than to another.

Ask two members, each from a different faction, to express the position of the other faction. That way, each member will feel that he/she has been understood by the members of the other faction.

On paper, the process just described may seem all too simple. However, with prayer, dialogue, and a spirit of reconciliation and discernment, you can reach a consensus on the areas of agreement and disagreement. Then you won't have to spend all your time arguing any more. You can move forward in the areas of agreement and live patiently with the areas of disagreement. You can even offer the handshake of peace and sing: "They'll Know We Are Christians by Our Love."

Handling Divisive Issues

 Our parish council had a big fight when we voted to close the school. It occurred during an open meeting which many

parishioners attended. There was shouting and name-calling,
resulting in many hurt feelings. The close vote for closing has left
our council divided and bitter. We have not met for six months.
The pastor feels it is impossible to put our council together again.
Since I am the chairperson, I would like to save this situation, but I
don't know what to do.

A Even the best families have fights. This isn't surprising. The early Christian communities also had some falling out among themselves (Acts 6:1-7). The Greek-speaking Jews had a fight with the Aramaic-speaking Jews over the distribution of relief to the poor. The widows of the Greek-speaking Jews were being neglected. The dispute had all the marks of discrimination. The problem was solved when the community selected seven men from the Greek-speaking Jews and "ordained" them for ministry to the widows.

When St. Paul went to Jerusalem, he "opposed Peter to his face" (Galatians 2:11). Between St. Paul and Barnabas, "there arose a bitter quarrel so that they separated from each other" (Acts 15:39).

Conflict is no scandal; unwillingness to forgive is. Because Christians have received forgiveness through Christ, every Christian community has the power and grace to heal its own wounds, to reconcile its divisions.

I would suggest that you and your pastor visit each member of the council individually. Initiate a dialogue. Admit your own share of the guilt for the division in the council. Then ask what you can do to reconcile and unify the council.

After you have visited all the councillors, you might invite them to your home for the celebration of the Eucharist. You could select Scripture readings which proclaim the truth that disciples of the Lord are those who have learned how to forgive. You might choose the parable of the unmerciful servant: (Matthew 18:21-35), "Lord, how often shall my brother sin against me and I forgive him?" Or you might decide on Luke 7:36-50. Here the sinful woman washes the feet of Jesus with her tears, and Jesus tells St. Peter: "He who is forgiven little, loves little."

During the celebration of the Eucharist, the pastor might expand the penitential rite and offer the handshake of peace to everyone present. The homily could stress the meaning of Christian brotherhood as symbolized by the breaking of the bread. The Prayer of the Faithful could accent the need for forgiveness and unity in the one body of Christ. The hymns could be chosen to express the same theme.

If you cannot resolve this conflict yourselves, you might bring in a third party, a member of a neighboring parish council. This would reduce the emotional element. At the same time, it would open the way to a more objective arbitration of the dispute.

I hope and pray that you will move heaven and earth to bring the present standoff to an end. When you have been reconciled with your brother, you will once again be able to bring your gifts to the altar.

Removing Undesirable Members

Q We have a man on our council who is promoting a divisive faction both in our council and in our parish. If he is allowed to remain on our council, he will wreck it. How do we go about unseating an undesirable member?

A Usually this problem can be prevented if the nominating committee also serves as a careful screening committee. Not everyone who presents him or herself as a candidate for the council should be allowed to run for election.

However, if a really bad apple slips through, you may be forced to remove him/her from the council. The constitution of St. Joseph's parish council of Huntsville, Alabama, states: "Any action by a member of the council which is considered detrimental to the best interest of the parish, or contrary to the established objectives of the parish, shall be considered cause for removal. The member involved in any such action shall have the opportunity to meet with the pastor and the council in closed session prior to removal from office. A two-thirds vote of the total council membership shall be required for removal."

One would hope that the need to remove a member from the council would be extremely rare. On the other hand, we need to be realistic. Vatican II didn't eliminate original sin.

Arbitrating Parish Council Disputes

Q Our diocesan guidelines say that the diocesan pastoral council has to arbitrate parish council disputes. We feel the *diocese should stay out of it. Our diocesan pastoral council has no credibility with the priests of the diocese anyway.*

A I vote for your diocesan guidelines. Most disputes will, of course, be settled at the parish level. However, given the reality of original sin, there may be rare cases when a council needs the help of an outside arbitrator.

The method of arbitrating council disputes varies from diocese to diocese. But most councils can appeal for help from at least one of four diocesan agencies: 1) the diocesan office for parish councils; 2) due process; 3) the diocesan pastoral council; and 4) the bishop.

Of the four systems, I favor the one in use in a small midwest diocese. There, the diocesan pastoral council has a Committee on Parish Affairs. This committee is composed of a pastor, a sister, and laity who have experience on parish councils. Its purpose is to support and encourage the formation and smooth operation of parish councils. When necessary, it also arbitrates council disputes. If it fails to resolve a particular dispute, the appeal goes to the bishop as the last resort.

It's true that some diocesan pastoral councils have little credibility. They were formed more "from above" than "from below." The priests, sisters, and parish councils were never consulted.

But the diocesan pastoral council's lack of credibility is a separate problem. It should be thoroughly discussed at the next meeting of your priest's senate.

Negative Attitudes of "Reformers"

Q *My wife and I and many of our friends are fed up with parish councils. From the start, the parish council seemed to bring out all the "authorities" on what was wrong with the church and with our parish in particular. The authority of the parish priest was their main target. They seemed to feel that, if they could eliminate his authority, then they could go on to greater things. Those of us who were reared Catholic (and proud of it!) were caught completely off guard. We could find little fault with the way the priest managed the parish, either financially or spiritually, but we were no match for the self-appointed reformers. Don't expect us ever to get involved in a parish council again.*

A One of the more common defects in parish councils today seems to be a lack of spiritual formation for this new apostolate. Councilors need to be prepared to suffer. They will suffer from their peers on the council, from the apathy of fellow parishioners, and from their own sinfulness. Councillors need to remember that they belong to a church of sinners. That's why Sunday Mass begins with a confession of sins. This penitential rite reminds us that we are a sinful people constantly in need of the Lord's mercy and redemption. We are not angels.

Councillors can be proud, uncharitable, authoritarian, and self-righteous. They can even accuse their peers of unworthy motivation. So, unless a follower of Christ is prepared to suffer both from his own sins and those of others, he ought not to participate in any apostolate in the church. Paul's letters give us many details about the agonies of the apostolate. However, Paul did not complain of his infirmities; he gloried in them. Suffering was, in fact, the glory of his apostolic work.

The letter quoted above implies that, "to get involved in a parish council," a parishioner first has to find fault with the way the priest manages the parish. The exact opposite should be the case. Parishioners should not become councillors because they "have a bone to pick." Rather, they should become involved because they are baptized and confirmed in the priesthood of the faithful, because, in the Spirit, they have their own gifts to offer to the church and, finally, because, as Christians, they share in the prophetic mission of Christ.

It is true that, in the past, it seemed as though pastors had complete responsibility to "manage" the parish. However, Vatican II plainly teaches "that pastors were not meant by Christ to shoulder alone the entire saving mission of the church." It is primarily at the parish level that laypersons can grow into their adult responsibilites in the mission of the church. Yet, all growth is conditioned by one's willingness to accept the growing pains of frustration, discouragement and suffering. It is called *the cost of discipleship.*

Dealing with a Clique

  We have a "lobby" of sorts in our council. There is a clique of people strongly oriented toward their own interest. They

always vote the same, no matter what the issue. So long as this condition continues we can't work together as a community. What should we do?

A Bring the conflict out into the open. First, talk to your pastor, just to make sure he is aware of the problem. Then call the chairperson of the agenda committee. Ask him/her to allow at least thirty minutes for "process evaluation" during the next meeting.

When the time comes for this evaluation, take a few moments for shared prayer. Then lead off the discussion with some comments on the need for trust, openness, and honesty in the council. After that, trust in the Spirit and express your feelings. Just say that you have the feeling there is a clique, a voting block, in the council. Be sure to cite some instances which you feel are clique activity. Don't make any judgments. Just express your *own* feelings. No doubt other councillors will support you by expressing their own feelings. Once the conflict is out in the open you will be able to deal with it.

If this is the first time you are dealing with conflict in the council, this kind of meeting may get a bit "heavy." If so, you might end the meeting with a brief Reconciliation Service. Select an appropriate Scripture reading, pray together, offer the handshake of peace and conclude with a hymn. If you have coffee and donuts after the meeting, be sure to talk to all the "clique" before you go home.

It's bad enough to have cliques in the parish, but it's worse to have them in the council. St. Paul came down hard on the first cliques which developed in the body of Christ in Corinth (1 Corinthians 1:10-13). We have to do the same. It's never a pleasant task, but all of us have some responsibility for "fraternal" correction. St. Thomas Aquinas teaches that subjects even have a responsibility to correct their superiors, for example, their bishops.

The Board of Education—Council

Q What is the relationship of the parish council to the board of education? How does the education commission of the council mesh with these two groups?

A The board of education is under the education commission which is, in turn, under the parish council.

The parish council, representing all the parishioners, is the top policy-making body in the parish. As such, it is responsible for the parish's total educational mission, which includes the baptized and non-baptized, adults and children, and public and Catholic school populations.

Generally, the education commission is simply one of the five or more council commmissions, which may include administration, worship, Christian service, family life, youth, and missions.

The education commission may have the most members and the largest budget, but it should not be separate from the council or compete with it. One of the purposes of the council is to unify the whole mission of the parish. It does this in part by reviewing and approving the budgets of all the individual commissions, including that of education.

CCD—Parochial School Breach

Q *We have a very dedicated and capable full-time religious education coordinator and a CCD program involving about three hundred students. So far, our religious education coordinator has not been accepted by the parochial school teachers as their religious instruction advisor. As so often happens, there is a deep split between our parochial school and our CCD program.*

In an effort to unify our parish community, after two months of discussion at our parish council meetings, we decided to stick our neck out for the Lord and attempt to get the two groups to work together. To do that, we decided to have the students of both groups, one grade at a time, take part in the weekend liturgy at one Mass. This involved some minimum participation, such as gathering around the altar at offertory time and bringing up the gifts. It meant that two or three teachers, both parochial and CCD, would work together. This would not have taken any school time nor involved any practice.

Our CCD teachers accepted our plan quite well, but our parochial teachers came unglued. We heard everything from "We don't have time," to "It's not in our contract," and "It's an affront to our professionalism." I'm thankful that my children aren't learning the kind of Christianity that was displayed at that council meeting.

We felt we had to start somewhere. Were we wrong in attempting to bring about some unity in our parish in this way? Do you have any suggestions or solutions for this kind of problem?

A I'm glad you stuck your neck out for the Lord. I'm sorry the parochial teachers came unglued.

One of the main functions of the parish council is to build the unity of the whole parish community. As in your case, this often means reconciling two factions. It's never an easy task. There are no sure-fire formulas. However, I feel you are moving in the right direction.

Perhaps your council could consider some other steps in the same direction. You might sponsor an appreciation dinner for all your CCD and parochial school teachers. Invite their husbands and wives, too. Ask the CCD and parochial school students to work together to provide entertainment during and after the dinner. As the CCD and parochial teachers break bread together and share wine at the same table, your split may begin to heal.

When you feel the time is right, your worship committee could invite all teachers to join the full council in celebrating a reconciliation service. Scripture readings would be carefully chosen to emphasize the unity of the Christian community. The council members could take the initiative in offering the Kiss of Peace to all the teachers.

Individual councillors could also make an extra effort to show their support for the teachers' ministry, both CCD and parochial. They could, on occasion, show up at the teachers' classrooms to ask: "Is there anything the council can do to help you in your teaching ministry?"

Building the unity of the whole parish is a year-round job. It doesn't just happen by itself. With the help of the Lord, your council has to make it happen.

Catholic School Ignores CCD

Q *I belong to the education commission of our council. We have problems with the school committee, which does not belong to the council. We have responsibility for adult education and for the religious instruction of our public high school and grade school children. The school committee is in charge of our own grade school. Yet we get no cooperation from the school committee members in the use of facilities, visual aids, and other* *materials. They say these materials belong to the Catholic school. How do other councils solve this problem?*

A If your council was formed after the school committee, it will not be easy to put the school committee "under" the council. Still, most other councils do it in one way or another. This brings the educational efforts together and reminds everybody that parish facilities, including visual aids, belong to *all* the people in the parish.

One parish council reorganized all its educational programs under one committee, the Committee on Christian Formation. This committee then sub-divided itself into CCD, school, adult education, pre-school, and special programs.

This committee on Christian formation, one of five other committees on the council, is also responsible for enrichment programs for teachers. It offers special programs for the formation of spiritual leadership. It conducts workshops for parish teachers, whether they function in school, CCD, or adult education classes.

The pastor of the parish reports that this reorganization succeeded because he replaced the word "education" with "formation." He says this gave everybody a chance to start from a new and broader base.

CCD Board vs. Council

Q *Does a parish council have power over decisions made by the parish CCD board? This question relates to our role as a decision-making council. Some time ago, the CCD board passed a resolution stating that, if parents or their representatives could not attend a special meeting to register their children and listen to a talk about the books to be used, their children would not be accepted for CCD classes. Some parents brought complaints to our council, saying that they never got the word and their children were being penalized. We passed a resolution asking the CCD board to relax its policy. They refused, saying they are supreme since they were instituted by the pope.*

A Normally, the parish council is the top policy-making and coordinating body in the parish. Many diocesan guidelines spell this out very clearly. Unless the parish council has such authority, it becomes just another committee with a "paper" existence.

However, your problem has several dimensions. First of all, it relates to the diocesan religious education department. Your diocesan office may have some policies regarding your specific problem. You might check that out first.

Second, the organizational linkage between your parish council and the CCD board appears to be rather weak. If your parish council is going to be an effective coordinating body, you need to have a good ongoing relationship with the other boards and committees in your parish. Ideally, a representative of your CCD board would be a member of your parish council and give reports about broad policy matters. Thus, your CCD programs could be coordinated through your education commission. If your council suddenly "lowers the boom" on the CCD board because of complaints from irate parents, it may be acting in a rather authoritarian manner. In other words, your problem pertains more to *method,* than to authority. If your authority is going to be an effective unifying service, it has to *earn* the respect of those it wishes to serve. Then it has to be channeled and used accordingly. A resolution can easily alienate the very ones whose cooperation you need.

Third, you need to check the by-laws of the CCD board to see if the policy they follow is within their competence. If not, the council might better concentrate on the by-laws than on a specific issue.

Fourth, you could check how many parents are upset. Parish councils shouldn't use a sledge hammer to pound a tack. If only three or four parents are complaining, it would be better to talk to them directly on a one-to-one basis.

Parish councils should not become the "complaint department" of the parish. Real problems cannot be ignored. Parish councils have to be sensitive to them, but they should devote most of their time to developing the board policies which will reduce complaints in the future. Most complaints can be handled in the smaller meetings of the council's committees or outside of council meetings.

Using the Pulpit

Q *In our parish, the chairman of the administration commit-*
tee, a man, speaks annually from the pulpit about the finan-
cial needs of the parish. Why cannot I, a woman, as head of the
Christian service commission, speak from the pulpit about our
needs?

A I see no reason why you, a woman, should not have an equal
right to speak from the pulpit. I know of no theological or
pastoral considerations which could justify discrimination on the
basis of sex.

Certainly, the finance chairperson shouldn't be the only
council member who speaks from the pulpit. This would convey the
impression that money is the major concern of the parish council.
This is not the kind of image a good parish council wants to project. The council shares in the total mission of the church. The major concern should be to proclaim and live the Gospel, especially
the Gospel of service.

COMMITTEES

Committee Representation

Q *We're revising our constitution. Why must the representative to the council always be the chairperson of the committee? We feel such a requirement is too restrictive.*

A I see no reason why the committee's representative to the council *has* to be the chairperson. Generally, the committee members elect their own chairperson. They are in the best position to know who is most competent to chair the meetings and to expedite the committee's business.

The representative to the council is elected to the council by the people of the parish. Assuming the elected councillor also serves on a committee, he/she can represent that committee whether he is chairperson or not. He can make reports and recommendations in the name of his committee.

Constitutions should allow some flexibility. The less detail, the better. They should not take away the freedom the Spirit has given us through Vatican II.

Non-Member Committee Chairpersons

Q *We are in the process of organizing our parish council and have come to an impasse in working out our constitution. Our problem (and we have strong support on both sides) is this: Should committee chairpersons sit on the council as members or should an elected council member be on each of the committees to bring a report of their work back to the council meeting?*

A We have followed the policy that the *elected* council members should be given high priority in the formation of constitutions and guidelines. They have a broad base of support from the people of the parish. Through them, the principle of representation becomes part of the parish decision-making process. They represent the voice of the people. They bring the people's needs to the meeting. Their status and responsibility should be respected. To undercut their position in any way would betray the parishioners who elected them.

For this reason, I suggest that committee chairpersons should not sit on the council as members. (I am assuming the committee chairperson was not elected by the parishioners.)

I would suggest that an elected member of the council be a member of each standing committee. He/she can then bring back a report of the committee's work to the council meetings.

Organizational patterns will vary from parish to parish. But basically, the committees should serve the council. They should gather the facts, do the necessary research, and prepare reports before the council meets. This is the homework which can best be done in small groups. This group can consult experts whose opinions could be incorporated in the reports. Such reports can then be attached to the agenda and mailed to council members well in advance of the meeting. The elected council member on the committee presents the report and acts as interpreter for the rest of the council members.

Meeting "Burn-Out"

Q *Our pastor expects* all committee members *to be present at all council meetings. We feel he's expecting too much. It's boring to sit there when you have no vote and no voice in the discussion.*

A Your pastor's expectations are a bit much. Too many meetings can stifle zeal and good will and can cause "burn-out." The council agenda should allow ten minutes to hear the opinions of any interested parishioner. After that, the discussion should be limited to the voting members. The council should receive the committee's input through a designated representative.

Of course, the chairperson should feel free to ask for opinions and information from outside experts who have special knowledge about specific issues being discussed.

The Bingo Committee

Q *On our council we have a standing committee for bingo. At every meeting we have to listen to long reports about the shortage of bingo workers and other problems. Some of us feel we*

*should simplify our committee system to eliminate the bingo com-
mittee. Others, including the pastor, feel the bingo committee
should be retained because bingo is an important parish activity.
What do you think?*

A I may incur the wrath of your pastor, but I feel your bingo
committee should be cut down a notch or two. It shouldn't
have equal status with your education, worship, or Christian service committees. Bingo, at best, is only a means to an end. It
shouldn't become the mission of the parish.

In response to your question, I feel the standing committees
should "stand for" the mission of the parish. They should be few
in number so that the council will not become top heavy with committees. Five to seven should be enough.

Committees for specific programs such as bingo should be
placed under standing committees. Such committees should report,
not to the full council, but to their standing committee. I suggest
you reduce your bingo committee to sub-committee status and put
it under the finance and administration committee.

Planning Committee Programs

Q *At the first meeting of our parish council, I was elected
chairperson of the parish worship committee. I don't know
what our committee should be doing. Our guidelines are not much
help. Can you help us get started?*

A First, you will need to select the members of your committee. Try to get "across the board" representation. This will
help you to keep in contact with the grass-root parishioners for
whom the liturgy is being celebrated. They will offer constant feedback on the effectiveness of various liturgical celebrations.

Then, select delegates from the performers of the liturgy,
who include priests, sisters, musicians, lectors, and ushers. Next,
select specialists, such as an artist, architect, dramatist, audio-
visual teacher, writer, and research scholar. You will need this kind
of talent to prepare good liturgies. You may need a total of twelve
or fifteen members on your committee.

Second, request a generous budget. The liturgy is an education which reaches more people than any other program in the
parish. It takes money to do it well. Good art, architecture, musi-

cians, and training programs do not come free.

Third, determine the goals and purposes of your committee. You might divide these into five categories: 1) self-education, 2) spiritual self-growth, 3) parish education, 4) community evaluation, and 5) liturgy preparation. These five divisions could determine your sub-committees.

Part of every meeting could be devoted to self-education. This could mean a speaker, a paper, a book report, a talk, or a filmstrip. It could mean subscriptions to current periodicals such as *Worship* (Collegeville, Minnesota) or *Newsletter* (Bishops' Committee on the Liturgy), or newsletter from your own diocesan liturgy commission.

Parish education could mean parish workshops, liturgical weekends, lectures, home study programs, a liturgical library, or a liturgy column for the parish bulletin or council newsletter.

Community evaluation could mean open forums and parish surveys. Brief questionnaires could gather feedback on the music, readings, homilies, art, and the handshake of peace. Special observers could evaluate baptisms, confirmations, funerals, weddings, and communal penances.

Fourth, devote some time each month to planning a Mass together. You might choose the Sunday celebration or some special event, such as a wedding anniversary, Thanksgiving, or Mother's Day.

Generally, the planners first decide on the theme of the Mass. Then they select appropriate readings from the lectionary. Next, they determine what alternatives and options are most expressive of the theme. They select the hymns and compose a Prayer of the Faithful which will reflect the current needs of the world, nation, community, and parish.

Christian Service Committee Needs

 I have been elected chairperson of the Christian service commission. Our commission meetings are going nowhere because we don't know what we should be doing. Do you have any suggestions?

A   Your motto might well be the words of Christ: "For the Son of Man Himself did not come to be served but to serve, and to give his life as a ransom for many." Christ washed the feet of his apostles to give an example of Christian service for all of us.

Specifically, you will need to identify the major social problems in your parish and in your community. Then you will need to educate your fellow parishioners about the social problems you have discovered. You will also need to enlist the help of professional resource people who can assist you in solving specific problems.

Before you try to solve social problems, your committee could first inform itself about the teaching of the church in matters of: 1) human relations; 2) economics; 3) politics—local, state, and national; 4) international life; and 5) the family. One helpful study-aid in these areas is Vatican II's *Pastoral Constitution on the Church in the Modern World.*

In helping the poor, the sick, and the aged, you will need to build good working relationships with other agencies, such as the city or county health department, United Way, Goodwill Industries, Alcoholics Anonymous, St. Vincent de Paul Societies, and Annettes. Your commission may need a member from the local police force, a physician, a lawyer, a counselor, and a member from the minority groups. A college or high school student would also be helpful.

One parish in Minnesota invited the parishioners "to help their brothers" by publishing the following list of service: 1) transportation to doctor or to church; 2) babysitting for mothers at day care centers; 3) housekeeping for mothers in hospitals or other emergency situations; 4) work with senior citizens programs; 5) caring for the sick in the parish; 6) visiting the sick at convalescent homes; 7) special services and problems—psychiatric and legal, drug addition and delinquency, divorcees and widows.

Problems will vary considerably from parish to parish. The challenge to your commission is to discover the problems and, in the light of the Gospel, to offer the appropriate Christian response.

PARTICULAR ISSUES

Invite Protestants?

Q   *During our last meeting, it was suggested that Protestants be invited to serve on our parish council. This caused a rather hot discussion. What do you think?*

A   The Vatican II *Decree on Ecumenism* provides us with some guidelines in this area. "Catholics," the decree states, "must assuredly be concerned for their separated brethren, praying for them, keeping them informed about the church, *making the first approaches towards them.*"

In another section, the same decree discusses the relations of separated brethren with the Catholic Church. "Cooperation among all Christians," according to the decree, "vividly expresses that bond which already unites them and it sets in clearer relief the features of Christ, the Servant. Such cooperation . . . should be ever increasingly developed. . . . "

Many forms of cooperation are possible in the application of Gospel principles to social life. In this matter, the same decree is quite specific: "Christians should also work together in the use of every possible means to relieve the afflictions of our times, such as famine and natural disasters, illiteracy and poverty, lack of housing, and the unequal distribution of wealth. Through such cooperation, all believers in Christ are able to learn easily how they can understand one another better and esteem one another more, *and how the road to the unity of Christians may be made smooth.*"

The scandalous divisions in the Christian church need to be reconciled. The wounds in the Body of Christ need to be healed. Hopefully, no parish council will fail to respond to this call of Vatican II.

Some form of Protestant participation in parish councils ought to be the accepted norm. Perhaps other faiths could be represented on the committee on ecumenism. Or they could be members of the Christian service commission. No doubt, the Thanksgiving clothing drive and aid to flood, earthquake or tornado victims could well be interfaith activities sponsored by an interfaith Christian service commission. Poverty, housing, race, divorce, delinquency and many other social apostolates really need the ministry of an interfaith team.

While Protestants could well be members of the working committees, I do not feel they should be voting members of the full council. In Catholic theology, the apostolate flows from the eucharistic celebration, hearing the Word and breaking bread together. The parish pastoral policies should come from those who celebrate the full Eucharist and so witness to a common faith.

Then, too, service on the council is a ministry. As such, it is accountable to the church. And this church is a very specific Catholic community. "Being Catholic" is one of the qualifications for serving as a minister in the Catholic Church.

Apartment vs. Rectory

Q *Our parish rectory is falling apart. Instead of spending a huge amount of money to build a new one, our council would like the pastor to live in an apartment near the church and school. His office would be in the school. He's for it, but the bishop is not. Since it's our money, do we have to go along with the bishop?*

A Yes, you probably do ... at least for the time being.

Councils are often surprised to discover how much control bishops have over their priests. Sometimes bishops may be following their own judgment and policies. Other times they may be applying the statutes of a diocesan synod. Then again, they may be interpreting the code of canon law.

Bishops who have a paternal style and who lean heavily on canon law have some precedent for close supervision of the conduct and the life-style of their priests. Here are a few examples from the clergy section of the Code of Canon Law: "Clerics are not allowed to wear a ring" (Canon 136). "Clergy must not play games of chance for money ... nor indulge in hunting" (Canon 138). "Clergy must keep away from theatrical performance, dances and shows ... which are unbecoming to clergy ..." (Canon 140). The Sacred Congregation of the Council, on January 10, 1920, declared that "the code of canon law does not give liberty to all the secular clergy to wear a beard, and that bishops may forbid it in their respective dioceses."

Of course, these canons are no longer enforced in many dioceses. Yet, the fact that they are on the books should alert councils to the possibility that an individual bishop may not allow his priests to live in an apartment.

At least one bishop feels priests should live near the church and the Blessed Sacrament to guard it against theft and vandalism. Another feels they should live in the rectory to be more available to their people.

Of course, bishops themselves are not of one mind on this question of clerical life-style. Many are changing their own living habits. Some are moving out of their episcopal "palaces," especially when they are located in the more affluent sections of the city. One bishop sold a huge bishop's residence with a swimming pool and moved in to a one-bedroom apartment.

Nowadays, many priests, including yours truly, are living in apartments. It's no big deal, but it has made me feel more responsible for my own life. I also feel a little closer to the day-to-day problems of the rest of the human race. It hasn't hurt me, for instance, to watch for sales, to clip coupons, and to note the price of hamburger at the check-out counter—not to mention doing my own laundry, washing the dishes, cleaning the apartment, and sharing jumper cables and shoveling cars out of the parking lot in the wintertime.

To get back to your question—your council's proposal makes a lot of sense. If you don't get anywhere in your dialogue with your bishop, you might appeal to your priests' senate or to your diocesan pastoral council, if you have one. If you succeed in bringing about a change in diocesan policy, you may be helping other parishes with a similar problem.

While I support your proposal, I can't really agree with one of your reasons: "It's our money." When we offer our gifts to the Lord at the offertory, we give up ownership over the gift. That's what it means to give a gift—to give control of the gift to someone else, in this case, to the church. If we say the offertory money remains *our* money, it's hardly a gift.

On the other hand, the gifts of the church are subject to the discernment of the church (that's us) regarding their most effective use in building the kingdom of God. So we (including the bishop) do have a voice in the disposition of the church's resources. That's not the same as saying: "It's our money." After all, the larger church (India, South America) may have a greater claim on the *church's* money.

Home Masses

Q *Is there anything in church law that says Masses can't be celebrated in parishioners' homes? Our pastor says he won't celebrate Mass in the home.*

A I suspect most dioceses do indeed have a "church" law regarding the celebration of Mass in the home. Some dioceses allow it; others don't. Naturally, some pastors interpret the law strictly while others "hang loose." Even if there's no diocesan law, I suspect that most bishops simply respect the pastoral judgment of the individual pastor.

Since I have offered Masses in the home, I can appreciate people wanting a home Mass for special occasions, such as the seventy-fifth birthday of a bed-ridden mother or father. Such home liturgies build up the spirit of community in a way which just isn't possible during crowded Sunday Masses.

With today's shortage of priests, however, it's quite understandable that an individual pastor would not celebrate Mass in the home as a regular practice. It's not unusual these days for a pastor to have a heavy commitment to special Masses on a weekly basis. He may offer Mass in the jail, in the convalescent home, in the school, in the convent, and for the charismatic prayer group. Add a funeral and a couple of weddings, and the pastor may be all "Massed-out" by the time he reaches the Sunday Mass schedule.

Of course, the Mass is only one of many forms of prayer. You might check with your liturgy committee or the diocesan liturgy office for home prayer services, such as the Advent wreath or renewal of baptismal promises, and so on. Numerous Bible services for special events are available at Catholic bookstores. Beginning with a parent, the members of the family could well exercise their baptismal priesthood and take turns in leading such prayer services in the home.

The Ordination of Women

Q *I see that the pope has come out with a declaration saying "no" to the ordination of women. Will this document settle the issue?*

A   I doubt it.

Since Vatican II, Pope Paul VI has issued encyclicals which say "no" to birth control and optional celibacy, but lively discussion still continues. No doubt the ordination of women will also be debated for many years to come.

Such free and open dialogue is a sign of life in the church. It's part of the process of discernment which often leads the church to a new understanding of itself and its mission. In their Pastoral Letter, *The Church in Our Day,* the United States' bishops remind all Catholics that they may be obliged in conscience to express their opinions: "The laity, and even more, the clergy by reason of their particular offices, are called to contribute their opinions on what concerns the good of the church; their call to do so may even oblige in conscience" (U.S. Catholic Conference, 1968, 72-73).

The church is very much like the human body. When one part of the body feels a pain, the whole body feels it. The healthy parts will, by various signs, report the hurt felt in another part of the body; for example, the face will grimace. In the same way, when the church feels a need or a hurt, it can't help but talk about it. The hurt will not go away merely because Rome says: "Go 'way."

A number of heavyweight theologians, who have discussed the question of women's ordination, conclude that there is no theological reason against it. Karl Rahner writes: "The practice which the Catholic Church has of not ordaining women to the priesthood has no binding theological character ... the actual practice is not a dogma; it is purely and simply based on a human and historic reflection which was valid in the past in cultural and social conditions which are presently changing rapidly."

The Declaration is not an encyclical and, therefore, is not signed by the pope. It is issued by the Vatican's Congregation for the Doctrine of the Faith, acting on a mandate from the pope. It is signed by Cardinal Franjo Seper, prefect of the Congregation, and by Archbishop Jerome Hamer, O.P., secretary.

The theology in the Declaration is, of course, the product of the Roman Congregation. No other schools of theology (German, American, and so forth) were consulted. There is no indication in the *Commentary* that any Bishops' Conferences or any women's organizations were consulted. The document is not infallible or irrevocable. Since it's not papal teaching, it can be changed.

A quick overview shows that the Roman Congregation did not take its task lightly. The document discusses most of the arguments usually presented in favor of the ordination of women. The *Commentary* shows an awareness of major developments, including the Ordination Conference held in Detroit in November, 1975.

Furthermore, it includes some pertinent references to the opinions of modern Scripture scholars. It notes, for instance, that 1 Corinthians 14:34-35 ("Women should keep silence in the churches") is a *late* interpolation. On the other hand, it is absolutely amazing that there is no reference to the findings of the prestigious Pontifical Biblical Commission which concluded there is nothing in the Scriptures against the ordination of women.

Now, to get to the theology of the text. In making its case for an exclusively male priesthood, the Declaration highlights the fact that Christ was of the male sex. It points out that the priest, while presiding at the Eucharist, acts in the person of Christ, "taking the role of Christ, to the point of being his very image ..." Basing its argument on St. Thomas, it concludes that "sacramental signs represent what they signify by natural resemblance." The person, therefore, who represents Christ must be of the same sex.

At first, this argument appears rather compelling. However, why is such a literal interpretation of the principle of representation really necessary, or even natural? Nancy Reagan doesn't have to be a man to represent a male president of the United States. Wives frequently represent their husbands and husbands represent their wives on rather important public missions. If, in our culture, the principle of representation is not bound to sex, why is sacramental representation bound to it?

Then, too, since the Council of Nicaea (325) the church has always taught that Christ assumed a *human* (not *male*) nature. The incarnation simply prescinded from individual differences, including that of sex. Accordingly, when, in our pre-Vatican II days, we recited the Latin Creed on Sunday, we said: "... et *homo* factus est" (and he [Christ] became a *human* person). We did not say: "... et *vir* factus est" (he became a *male* person).

Finally, there is no doubt that Christ in his *risen* state and in his present saving activity (including his priestly activity) is not bound by the limitations of sex. The activity of the kingdom of God breaking into the present world is simply of a higher order.

"For in the resurrection they neither marry nor are given in marriage, but are like the angels in heaven" (Matthew 22:30).

The Declaration also highlights the fact that the constant tradition of the church has been against the ordination of women. Now, no theologian worth his/her paycheck will lightly dismiss the weight of such a long tradition in the church.

On the other hand, the tradition of the past is not an absolute norm for the future. The church has often changed its own tradition. A few examples may jar the memory a bit. In its early history, the church taught that it was impossible to receive the sacrament of reconciliation more than once in a lifetime. As late as the thirteenth century, Pope Innocent III taught that Jews should "be forced into servitude" and "should be made to wander homeless on the face of the earth." Pope Clement V (fourteenth century) taught that it was sinful to accept interest on a loan of money. Pope Nicholas V (fifteenth century) excommunicated anyone who opposed the practice of "reducing Negroes to perpetual slavery." Certainly, the difference between the Councils of Trent and Vatican II represents a serious shift in the church's tradition.

It should be evident from these examples that obedience to tradition does not consist in a literal adherence to the church practice of the past. Rather, it requires an acceptance, in faith and obedience, of the guidance of the Spirit who "blows where he will." It calls for the gift of discernment "given to every believer." It requires a constant reference to the work of Christ and to the Gospel's *new* demands in view of new needs and new "signs of the times."

We may have to wait until Vatican III to see the ordination of women in the Catholic Church. Or again, we may never see it. But I do hope we never see a Declaration which tries to put an end to the fruitful dialogue that in our time began with Vatican II.

Success with Adult Education

Q   I don't have a problem. I just have some good news to share. Our council voted to send our adult education coordinator and our youth minister to Rome to study at the Angelicum University. They are husband and wife. He's studying for his doctorate in theology; she, for her master's.

We voted to grant them a $3,000 scholarship. In addition, we have sponsored a bingo party for them. The Knights of Columbus has sent a check. Many ordinary parishioners have contributed to the cause. The whole thing has mushroomed. Our parish council started it all, by voting for the scholarship.

A That sure is good news. More and more councils seem to be willing to spend some money for adult education. That's a welcome shift from the child-centered parishes of yesteryear. It's a sign, too, that councils are moving beyond the nuts and bolts of maintenance and are becoming more concerned about the parish's most important resource—people.

Thanks for sharing the good news. My hat is off to you and to your council.

Children's Masses

Q *Our liturgy committee wants a Children's Mass every Sunday at ten o'clock. Some of our single parishioners have complained about the mandatory Children's Mass, especially about its projected time. What do you think?*

A I would suggest you conduct a liturgy survey of all the parishioners to find out how many really want a Children's Mass on Sunday. Then, during your next parish forum, offer some information about the liturgical aspects of the question. Be sure to allow plenty of time for free, open discussion. It's quite possible your complaining parishioners make up a very small percentage of the total parish.

In the meantime, be ready to consider alternatives, such as a Children's Mass in the school or on Saturday evening, or no Children's Mass at all. In large city parishes, it's tough to organize the Mass-going habits of adults in favor of children.

Kiss of Peace

Q *I am on the liturgy committee of our parish council. We received letters from some parishioners requesting that we drop the handshake as a sign of peace during Mass. At least half the people simply refuse to shake hands. We feel everybody should do it, or it should be dropped entirely. It causes much talk and commotion during Mass, disturbing those who want to pray. Still, the priests want to keep the handshake. What should we do?*

A Many of us are used to "Jesus and I" prayer, even in the community worship of the liturgy. We do not easily incorporate the horizontal, the fraternal dimension into our worship. In the past, silence in church was a sign of piety. It was a sign of reverence for Jesus in the tabernacle. So, while silence became a virtue in itself, it also provided a convenient excuse for not relating to our neighbor.

Silence, of itself, is neither good nor bad. "Talking in church" could be a prayer if, while shaking hands, you tell your wife how sorry you are that you fought with her last night. It would also be edifying to actually tell your neighbor that you are praying for her sick daughter.

Regarding the handshake, why is it necessary that either everybody or nobody do it? Do we have to have a militaristic conformity during the liturgy? The ordinary family meal reveals a great diversity of eating habits. It does not resemble an army on the march.

If the handshake has no internal meaning for a person, it would be a mockery of the liturgy to force him or her to go through "empty motions" just to achieve uniformity. It is more important that worship be honest and authentic.

Have the priests really explained the meaning of the handshake?

Have you taken a survey of all the parishioners to find out why the people resist this practice? Perhaps they need education and motivation. However, we can't expect everyone to respond with equal enthusiasm to every liturgical sign.

Besides, we have to admit realistically that there will always be some people in those back pews who don't come to church to get involved. They simply want the "Mass of Non-involvement" to satisfy their obligation.

However, if you keep the handshake, there is at least the possibility that these passive parishioners may yet be moved by this sign of forgiveness and reconciliation. As a sign, it is offered as a grace which can be accepted or rejected. Even if it is rejected, it remains grace.

Dancing During Liturgy

Q *I belong to the liturgy committee of our parish council. We prepare a special teenage liturgy for our high school CCD*

*students. We have had some disagreements about the liturgical
dance which has been suggested for this Mass. At a neighboring
parish, a high school girl, dressed in jeans, danced in the sanctuary.
This caused a lot of talk. Some of us feel that's going too far, turn-
ing the church into a dance hall and distracting the people from
their prayers. We would appreciate your opinion.*

A   The dance has a long history as a form of religious expres-
sion. In Exodus 15:20, Miriam, the prophetess, took up a
timbrel and led the women in a dance. They were praising Yahweh
who had led them through the Red Sea. In 2 Samuel 6, David
danced before the ark of God, "whirling around before Yahweh
with all his might."

The liturgical dance is also a part of our own Christian tradition. "Throughout almost all centuries," concludes Hugo Rahner,
"clergy and people have wound sacred dance around the hard and
sober core of the liturgy." In the early centuries, Christians
celebrated the vigils of martyrs by dancing in the church or at the
martyr's tomb. St. Ambrose said, "The dance is spiritual
applause."

The liturgical dance was condemned by local councils of
Toledo (589) and again by the Council of Wurzburg (1298).
However, a close look at the decrees indicates the councils condemned, not the dance as such, but the low moral tone of the
festivities. At any rate, the liturgical dance continued.

In the Middle Ages, the dance was restricted mainly to the
feasts of Christmas and Easter. It was joined more closely to formal worship. On Easter Day, clerics danced in praise of Christ, the
Risen Sun. The ritual of the Church of Besancon in France states
that "... on Easter Day there is a dance in the cloister or, if the
weather is rainy, in the center of the church."

Even to this day in the Cathedral of Seville, the Spanish
dance before the Blessed Sacrament on the feast of Corpus Christi.

Daniel Kister (*Worship,* December 1971) concludes that
"the dance belongs to a people having the assurance of the incarnation and the promise of the resurrection .... It particularly recommends itself to Christian worship today. For Christians are today
beginning to affirm the human body after centuries of trying to
deny it."

In spite of the silent churches of the past, we Catholics have prayed with our bodies for a long time. Processions, standing, sitting, kneeling, and striking the breast are all forms of prayer. The dance is only another form of bodily prayer. If the liturgy is truly a *celebration* of God's saving deeds, then we ought to expect singing and dancing.

No doubt, the liturgical dance can be abused. But if it serves the liturgy, if it expresses the prayer of people, it can be a holy act of communal worship.

Sisters Leave School

Q During our last council meeting, the pastor announced that three of our sisters had chosen to leave our school to take up other work. He said the superior general would not send any replacements because the sisters were free to pick their own jobs and assignments. Why are the sisters leaving our schools and our children?

A The sisters report that there are a wide variety of reasons for choosing their own apostolate and for leaving the schools.

In the past, sisters were bound to a classroom assignment because their community had a commitment to staff a certain number of schools. The needs of the school for teachers were primary; the unique charisms, talents, and education of the individual sisters were secondary. Thus, a sister with a degree in nursing had to teach mathematics in the third grade. "We were really being used to fill a slot," one sister reports. "No one cared what unique personal ministry we could offer to the church."

In the past, many sisters had no degrees. Since they simply had teaching certificates, they were not prepared to do anything except teach grade-school children. They simply had no other options.

Further, many religious communities had rather narrow goals and rather narrow views of their role in the total apostolate of the church. In practice, they were oriented to children.

All of this is changing. Many sisters are more aware that "each has her own gift for the upbuilding of the church." They want to be true to the talents God has given them. For them, this is more surely God's will than simply filling an empty slot in a school.

Many religious communities have broadened their apostolates. Religious communities have moved into full-time campus ministry, parish ministry, adult education, public school teaching, and the role of parish secretary. The nursing sister may soon have a full-time ministry to all the convalescent homes in a given parish or city.

This shift into diverse ministries for sisters has caused some misunderstanding at the parish level. Some sisters have tried to clear up the confusion by meeting with the parents of their CCD students. Other sisters have conducted small group meetings in the homes of the parishioners to explain their new approach to the apostolate.

Most sisters agree that the 80's will see more and more sisters in adult education. For this reason, many sisters are getting degrees in theology and religious education. It's all part of the sisters' response to changing needs of the church in our times.

Into Political Areas?

Q *During our last parish council meeting, the deanery representative of the Council of Catholic Women gave a talk. She urged us to write to our congressman, asking him to veto the bill authorizing two billion dollars for a federal child-care program. This caused quite a discussion during our meeting. Some of us felt that a parish council should stick to church affairs and should not get into politics. What do you think?*

A The dictionary says "politics is the science or art of government." It does not say it is evil, profane, or "out of bounds" for Christians. No doubt it could become evil and un-Christian if it is deprived of Christian presence and Christian conscience. This could happen if all Christians "stick to church affairs."

Through the centuries, popes have written encyclicals on such "political" problems as labor, poverty, war, peace, communications, abortion, and euthanasia. Vatican II stated plainly that the church "has the right to pass moral judgments, even on matters touching the political order ...." In defending the conscientious objector, the council fathers recommended that, "laws make humane provisions for the case of those who, for reasons of conscience, refuse to bear arms ...."

Bishop Dozier of Memphis, Tennessee, in a pastoral letter, pledged his support "to any young man of draft age who refuses to serve in the military because he conscientiously objects to war and killing." Evidently, popes and bishops do not just "stick to church affairs."

The federal child-care bill could have rather serious effects on the holiness of family life. It seems altogether normal that a parish council would try to defend the Christian values threatened by such a bill. It is the business of the church and of parish councils to shed the light of the Gospel on the events of our times. This may mean "getting out of church" and into "politics."

Right-to-Life Programs

Q *Our parish council, at the suggestion of the pastor, has asked me, as chairman of the Christian Service Commission, to take charge of the Right-to-Life campaign. This kind of involvement is all new to me. What should I do?*

A   Your apostolate could be directed toward the Catholic community and toward the civic community.

You will need help, so begin with the concerned people on your commission and in your own parish. Once you have recruited some helpers, you will need information and educational materials. Go to your diocesan office of Catholic Charities or to your Right-to-Life Committee, if one exists. Such offices will have books, pamphlets, filmstrips, brochures, names of speakers, and other aids. Pick up all the materials you can, and send the bill to the finance committee of the council.

First, direct your effort to your own parish. Show the filmstrip at the Sunday Masses. Get a Catholic nurse or doctor to speak from the pulpit on *Right-to-Life* Sunday. Select an appropriate reading from the Gospel, and prepare a special Prayer of the Faithful.

Next, show the filmstrip at the meetings of the Altar Society, Holy Name and Knights of Columbus. After each showing, have a question and answer period with good resource persons at your side. Each time, ask for a donation of time, talent, or money. Your goal is to share this responsibility with your parish community.

Second, team up with the other parish councils in your city. Form a city wide Right-to-Life Committee. Plan a program of education for this committee. During this time, keep in contact with your diocesan office. Ask the bishop and the priests of your city to sign a joint letter to help bring the whole Catholic community together.

Third, move into the civic community. Contact the doctors, sisters, nurses, and administrators at local hospitals and convalescent homes. Contact your state representatives and the public officials in your community. Don't by-pass the Boy Scout and 4-H leaders, the staff members of the local home for retarded children, the public school principals, or other interested persons.

Then you will be ready to start your education program. Buy a full page ad in the daily paper, which should be paid for and signed by the priests, ministers, doctors, nurses, and other professionals in the city. Contact the Kiwanis, Rotary, and other groups to find out if you can speak at their meetings. Contact your local television station to find out if they will give you free time as a public service. Many public schools will allow outside speakers in school if the request comes from the students. Work this through your high school CCD students.

Drug Rehabilitation Efforts

Q *I am on the Christian service committee of our parish council. We have received a request to open up a drug rehabilitation center. Many of our high school students are hooked on drugs.*

We have two problems. First, some of us feel that the parish council should not get involved in secular problems such as drugs. Second, even if we decide to tackle this problem, we don't have the money to staff such a center. With the rising school costs, we are having a tough time keeping our heads above water. Our council has come to an impasse on this.

A The Vatican II *Decree on The Laity* talks about "the apostolate of the social milieu." The *Decree* goes on to say that "the laity ... need the kind of fraternal charity which will lead them to share in the living conditions, labors, sorrows, and hopes of their brother ... They need a full awareness of their role in building up society ...."

In Vatican II's *The Church Today,* we read that "a special obligation binds us to make ourselves the neighbor of absolutely every person, and of actively helping him when he comes across our path." "In promoting the common good," Christians must be concerned about "murder, genocide, abortion, euthanasia, prostitution, imprisonment, and whatever insults human dignity." The same passage reminds us that "God forbids us to make judgments about the internal guilt of anyone."

The Vatican II documents do not specifically mention drugs or rehabilitation centers. Yet the social ills which are mentioned give a sufficient idea of the area of the Christian's apostolate to and in the world. Drugs seem to come under the "signs of the time" calling for a Christian response. This should help solve the first part of your problem.

I have no solution for your money problem. However, you might explore some other areas. First, have you contacted the Catholic Charities' office of your own diocese? They may have started some program in your own city. Second, have you talked to neighboring parishes who may have the same problem? You may not need "to go it alone." Third, have you contacted your city health department? Since this is a community problem, your parish council might best cooperate with "all men of good will" in your community. Such cooperation with the civic community may be far more practical and effective. Besides, cooperation in itself is a powerful Christian witness to the fraternal charity which prompts us to share the labors and sorrows of our brothers and sisters.

Intercommunion

Q I am a member of the ecumenical committee. We have sponsored a number of prayer meetings with the neighboring Lutheran parish. Recently, during the Week of Prayer for Christian Unity, the Lutheran minister read the Scriptures during our special liturgy and also received Holy Communion. This sharing of the Eucharist caused considerable discussion during our next council meeting. The whole problem was then referred to our committee "for study and policy recommendation." What is the status of intercommunion at the present time?

A The problem of intercommunion is rather complex. It's certainly too complicated to attempt any kind of complete answer here.

However, a few comments may get you started on your study. *The Ecumenical Directory,* published on May 14, 1967, tries to safeguard simultaneously the integrity of ecclesial communion and the good of souls. On May 25, 1972, the Secretariat for Promoting Christian Unity issued an *Instruction Concerning Cases When Other Christians May Be Admitted to Eucharistic Communion* in the Catholic Church.

This *Instruction* explains that admission to Catholic eucharistic communion is permitted when it "is confined to particular cases of those Christians who have a faith in the sacrament in conformity with that of the church, who experience a serious spiritual need for the eucharistic sustenance, who for a prolonged period are unable to have recourse to a minister of their own community, and who ask for the sacrament of their own accord; all this provided that they have proper dispositions and lead lives worthy of a Christian .... Further, even if those conditions are fulfilled, it will be a pastoral responsibility to see that the admission of these other Christians to communion does not endanger or disturb the faith of Catholics."

Although the *Instruction* does not speak to your particular situation, it gives some idea of the principles involved. The official accent seems to be on *particular* cases. No doubt, it is up to the local church to exercise a pastoral judgment regarding specific cases.

The question of intercommunion is related to at least three theological problems. First, what kind of *union* must exist before it is expressed through a sacramental celebration? Whose version of unity decides the issue? Is unity defined in legal terms of a visible society? Or is unity primarily a bond of faith and love in the mystery of Christ?

Second, whose definition of *church* is normative? Vatican II tells us that Protestant communities can truly be called ecclesial. Although they don't share *full* communion, these ecclesial communities share with us certain common elements, such as "the word of God; the life of grace; faith, hope and charity, along with other interior gifts of the Holy Spirit ...." Vatican II decided that the church is a mystery and therefore can't be defined. The question is, how and when is an imperfect, though real, communion celebrated sacramentally?

Third, what is the relationship between Eucharist and ministry? If Vatican II accepted the validity of some Protestant communities, did it *implicitly* accept the validity of their ministries? If so, are not their eucharistic celebrations also valid?

There is a good possibility, at least, that the ministries of Lutheran churches are valid. In 1970, the Roman Catholic theologians who participated in the Lutheran-Catholic Dialogue concluded "... in our study we have found serious defects in the arguments customarily used against the validity of the eucharistic ministry of the Lutheran Churches. In fact, we see no persuasive reason to deny the possibility of the Roman Catholic Church recognizing the validity of their ministry. Accordingly, we ask the authorities of the Roman Catholic Church whether the ecumenical urgency flowing from Christ's will for unity may not dictate that the Roman Catholic Church recognize the validity of the Lutheran ministry and, correspondingly, the presence of the body and blood of Christ in the eucharistic celebrations of the Lutheran Churches."

In view of the above, it seems that the annual Week of Prayer for Church Unity could be one appropriate time for inter-communion between Lutherans and Catholics. In this way, Lutherans and Catholics could celebrate at least the unity of faith and love which has already been achieved.

It's quite probable that Jesus will be present in such celebrations, praying once again: "Father, may they be one in us as you are in me and I in you."

Council Member Spirituality

Q   As a pastor with a new parish council, I have become aware of the great need for spiritual formation of council members. Do you have any suggestions?

A   You might team up with your neighboring pastors and take your council to a weekend workshop at a retreat house. Such a workshop could combine content and experiences. One schedule for such a workshop included the following: 1) liturgical experience (communal penance and special liturgy); 2) development of communication skills; 3) theology of the church and parish; 4) the pastoral mission of the church; and 5) group dynamics experiences.

Industrial and business managers have recognized the value of such workshops and conferences for their top executives. If we expect responsible lay leadership in the church, we will need to spend some money to develop the charisms and talents of our parishioners.

However, Christian formation is not just a weekend experience. Every meeting is an opportunity for spiritual growth. Some councils open each meeting with a brief scripture reading followed by an exchange of personal reflections. Others read pertinent passages from Vatican II documents. Some councils occasionally celebrate the liturgy in the home of a council member.

Still spiritual formation is not simply a question of "exercises." It's an ongoing process. The pastor, as prophet in the midst of his people, is called to preach the Word "in season and out of season." He is servant to the Word at every moment of the council meeting. This is his witness, his special contribution to the formation of a truly Christ-centered council.

Training New Councillors

Q *Our parish is located in an area of high mobility. People are constantly moving in and out, so we have lots of resignations. This means we always have to train new people on the council. It takes most of our meeting time. How do we work through this problem?*

A You may have to live with it, but it's not all bad. Training and educating new councillors is part of the mission of every parish council. You may be forming, inspiring, and motivating new lay ministers for other parishes and missions. Your council may, in fact, be a training school for ministry for the larger church.

If you have many people moving in, I suspect some of them have served on parish councils in other parishes. Recruit them for your council. They will at least not be *totally* new to the council experience.

Also, if necessary, you might amend your constitution so councillors will serve for three rather than for two year terms. That way only a third of your members will be new in any year because of elections.

Then, too, select some of your candidates from your council's committees. They will be rather familiar with your council through the committee system.

Finally, conduct a special orientation session for your new councillors after elections. Let them get all their questions out. Then you can get down to business during your actual council meetings.

Orienting New Members

Q *Every year half of our council is elected new. Our constitution limits members to two-year terms. We feel our turnover is too quick. It takes about a year for the new members to catch on. The result is that our council programs lack continuity. We spend most of our meetings training new members and bringing them up to date. Any suggestions?*

A First, I would suggest you amend your constitution to allow members to be elected to three-year terms. Then stagger your elections so that only one-third of the council will be elected new in any given year.

Second, I would suggest you conduct three special orientation sessions for the new members. Such sessions provide the new members an opportunity to talk about the hopes, gifts and talents they bring to the council. At the same time, they can ask questions about the functions of the council and its committees. Such sessions will save you all kinds of time during the actual meetings. The new members will get in the swing of things much faster. The council can then get on with the business at hand.

Orientation sessions have a fourfold purpose: 1) to provide input with discussion on the theory of the church and the parish council; 2) to practice the dynamics of an actual council meeting; 3) to pray together; and 4) to help new councillors get acquainted with each other.

CLERGY/RELIGIOUS ON COUNCIL

Role of Sisters

Q *What is the role of a sister on a parish council?*

A A number of interviews with sisters on parish councils yielded a wide variety of viewpoints. However, many sisters agree on certain core issues.

Sisters, first of all, feel they belong on councils. "We are Christians and members of the parish like everyone else," one sister commented. "We do not like to be isolated from the life of the parish community."

Second, the sisters feel they have a good knowledge of parish conditions through the children in school and through frequent contacts with the parents. Because of this experience, they can contribute information which is valuable to council decisions.

Third, sisters feel they have a responsibility to help in the development of adult leadership in the parish. They feel their education should benefit not only the children, but also the adults. Councils provide an excellent opportunity for sisters to share their experience in teaching and leadership roles with the laity of the parish.

Fourth, sisters frequently mention that their participation in councils is one aspect of larger developments in the postconciliar church. The updating and pastoral adjustments of religious communities have prepared the people to accept sisters in active parish involvement. More and more, sisters prefer to extend their apostolic work beyond the four walls of a classroom. In the future, more and more sisters will become full-time pastoral associates.

Finally, sisters prefer to serve on the commission where their training and experience will have maximum influence. One sister commented, "They always want the sisters to be secretaries because they are women with nice handwriting. We want to serve on liturgy, education, and Christian service commissions."

Some sisters expressed the hope that they could plan special liturgies for young adults through a liturgy committee rather than through a one-to-one meeting with the pastor. Other sisters reported that, since Vatican II, religious communities are more favorable to their total parish involvement.

Councils have highlighted the need for sisters to develop their leadership skills and to maintain good rapport and communications with the parish priests.

Several sisters were impressed by the team approach to the parish ministry. With increasing frequency, sisters are asking to serve on such pastoral teams. No doubt, the role of sisters on councils will continue to develop as the pastoral methods of the church adjust to "the signs of the times."

Priest Membership

Q Our interim constitution and by-laws restrict priest membership in the parish council to the pastor and two associates. One of the points in the discussion of our proposed new constitution is this: should all three associates be on the council or should the present constitution remain unchanged on this point? Some feel that adding the third associate would "load the council in favor of the establishment." Others feel all the priests would be more effective in the conduct of parish life if they had a vote on the council.

A   To answer your question directly, I feel all full-time associates should be voting members of the parish council. First, associates offer a full-time ministry to the people of the parish. For this ministry, they are accountable to God. But they are also accountable to the people of the parish. The meeting of the parish council is one way in which they can render an account of their stewardship as ministers of God's mysteries.

Second, associates need to be members of the parish council for their own growth and pastoral enrichment. By listening to the councillors, they will discover the true needs of the parishioners. They need this feedback so they can make the proper adjustments in their pastoral ministry. This two-way communication is the lifeblood of a good parish council.

Third, the associates, by their presence, give prophetic witness to the Word of God. The council meetings give the priest a chance to apply the priorities of the Gospel to real, concrete situations. Often this is not possible in the pulpit.

Fourth, the associates can be available to offer support and spiritual guidance before, during, and after meetings. Sometimes this simply means they show a willingness to share the trials and frustrations of councillors who are discovering the apathy of the rest of the parish.

Fifth, they may need some human support to sustain their own ministry. The council meetings give the priests a feeling of belonging to a team. The zeal and dedication of fellow councillors can be a boost to their morale. Many priests spend most of their office time dealing with alcoholics, delinquents, marriage failures, and so forth.

Your comment about "loading the parish council in favor of the establishment" assumes a polarization will exist in the council. One should hope that no constitutions will ever acknowledge or promote factions for or against any "establishment."

Regarding the associates' voting patterns, we can assume their votes represent a mature judgment on the issue being discussed and not a reaction for or against the "establishment." Experience shows that associates' votes simply are not predictable on the basis of any "establishment" bias.

Another solution to your problem might be to add more lay members to the council. At-large members could be elected for every three hundred families. This might provide the necessary lay representation.

Priests' Ministry

Q *How does the priest's ministry today relate to parish councils? What is the most serious adjustment for an old-timer?*

A It is, of course, a privilege to minister to the People of God. However, the priest's ministry is a service which is subject to review. He needs to render an account of his stewardship; he needs to show he is worthy to continue his service. Also, he needs to know if it is still useful to the People of God. Without such a review, he runs the risk of having his service rejected.

Today's pastor doesn't need to read *The National Catholic Reporter* to discover that today's Catholics have little tolerance for secrecy. If the laity are being asked to make a responsible contribution to the decision-making process, they rightly feel they should have all the facts. They expect and deserve honesty and openness from all the members of the council, especially the pastor.

American Catholics are more conditioned by the public media than by church policies. Television cameras peer into the government decision-making process. Since the media are sensitive to people, they concentrate both on the reactions to, and the actions of, our public servants. This process of the democratic system is in the American Catholic's blood. This is the mindset many Catholics bring to the church system. To them the priest is very much a public servant.

Perhaps this is another reason that large numbers of Catholics feel the church needs an internal evaluative system. They do not feel this way because they are anti-clerical, as some threatened priests seem to think, but because they feel this is part of the process in the responsible up-building of a postconciliar church. If I have any ability to read "the signs of the times," it is a matter of great urgency that all priests be prepared to relate to such a system. Parish councils could well perform this service.

Today's pastor needs a deep faith, a real trust, in the good will of the council members. His leadership ability and his ministry will improve considerably if he offers it regularly to the people for evaluation. His particular service is always a tentative offer. He is ready to die, to give it up, if in that way he serves the people better. This disposition "to give it up" will free him from the suspicion of self-interest, of imposing himself and his office on the people by the force and weight of an institution. Through evaluation, he will *earn* his leadership position.

In the future, the priest's leadership ability will be tested by parish councils. This test is the price of true leadership. This will be a severe trial unless the priest learns a lesson from the behavioral sciences, unless he is open to the Spirit in the church, unless he is disposed to risk and revise his pet answers. And this may well be the most serious adjustment for some "old-timers."

YOUTH

Inactive Youth Committee

Q *Our youth commission never got off the ground. The college student who was elected chairman just never did anything. Should the council appoint a replacement?*

A The parish council should ask for the resignation of the college student "who never did anything." Then, the parish council may either conduct a special election or appoint another person to complete the unexpired term.

No commission should be "dead." The whole body of the council suffers when one commission is inactive. Such a commission should either be eliminated or activated. A crippled commission has a demoralizing effect on the rest of the members. Besides, the growth of all commission members, like an organism, should be simultaneous in all areas.

Bored Teenagers on Council

Q *We have two teenagers on our council, but they are bored to death. What can we do to get them interested and involved in our council?*

A First, you might initiate an honest dialogue with your teenagers. It may be that you are spending too much time on finances or the nuts and bolts of running the parish plant. This gets no response from today's youth.

Second, you might invite the two teenagers to start a coffee house. A meeting at St. Peter Church in St. Cloud, Minnesota reported the following coffee house activities: slide presentation; folk singing groups; movies; a barbecue; and some very good discussions. "The students decided," the report continues, "they want to be financially independent. If they need funds, they will raise them."

Young Life Program

Q *The youth committee of our council is starting a youth group. We would like very much to follow the* Young Life *program. Can you give us more information?*

A *Young Life* is a nonsectarian program, founded in 1941 by Jim Rayburn, a Protestant minister from Gainesville, Texas. It's neither an organized church, nor a substitute for church. Although it's not sponsored by any special church, Catholic or Protestant, it encourages its members to join a local church and to participate fully in the life of the parish or congregation.

Young Life serves the teen-age population. It's active in over three hundred communities in America, Canada, and several overseas countries. The program has a paid staff of seven hundred full-time and part-time workers, and over 3,500 people serve as volunteers.

Staff people are required to have a seminary degree or to complete the academic program for a Master of Arts in Theology through the Young Life Institute. Club leaders are trained in counseling and leadership skills.

A *Young Life* club is an informal meeting, held one evening a week, usually in the home of one of the members. The parents serve as hosts. The meetings may begin with group singing of popular songs, followed by spiritual and Gospel songs. A humorous skit may come next. Then an adult leader gives a ten minute talk on God, Christ, sin, redemption or some aspect of the Christian life. A casual, informal discussion ensues, sometimes with pizza and coke. There are no club dues and no signed memberships. The main purpose of the club is to foster good relationships with caring adults. The teenagers come to the club to learn from adults. Sometimes groups are segregated, so that girls will be free to talk to women leaders and boys with men.

"We get some kids who have been turned off by the church," reports Lillian Runnion, a staff leader from Orlando, Florida. "Catholic high schools," says Ms. Runnion, "are very cooperative. We frequently work with the faculty and the Catholic chaplains."

For more information write to Young Life Headquarters, P.O. Box 520, Colorado Springs, CO 80901.

Youth Representation

Q *Our steering committee has been asked to develop guidelines for the formation of a parish council. Some of us are in favor of a youth commission. Others say parish councils should be strictly for adults. Still others think that teenagers should have some representation on all the commissions, but that there is no need for a special youth commission. We are really hung up on this and need help.*

A I wonder if you have asked the opinions of the youth themselves.

Certainly, teenagers ought to have some role in the work of the parish council. They have much to offer. They are usually more sensitive to the "signs of the times." Since they belong to the "now generation," they may have some insights the adults need very badly. "Their heightened influence in society," according to Vatican II, demands of them a proportionately active apostolate ...." "... they are impelled by a zest for life ... and they yearn to play their part in the social and cultural life."

The form of teenage participation in parish councils seems to vary from parish to parish. Some councils have, in fact, formed a special youth commission. Others, however, bring the youth into all the commissions and reject the special commission approach.

Some teenagers resent the special youth commission because it simply structures the "generation gap." It also excludes them from the adult discussions of the other commissions in which they have a real interest. They do not like to be put into their own place, as if they were selfishly concerned only with their own teenage problems.

If you create a commission for every special interest group, your council could become unwieldy. How about the senior citizens? The migrants? Widows? Widowers? Divorced people? The list of special groups could be long in some parishes.

Generally, I am in favor of creating commissions in terms of functions or services rather than in terms of types of people served. This seems to be more in tune with the "variety of ministries" doctrine taught in *The Constitution on the Church*. It offers a greater challenge to develop a broader view of the needs of the whole parish community. It should prevent that vested interest and self-serving mentality which creeps into so many of our parish organizations.

Small Parishes

Council in Mission Parishes

Q *We have a mission parish. So we have no resident pastor. Do you think we could start a parish council anyway?*

A Yes. I'm assuming that some neighboring pastor has responsibility for your mission. If that's the case, I would see no reason why you couldn't have your own council. Of course, you would have to tailor it to your own needs in terms of size, kinds, and number of committees.

In setting up your council, you will need to stay in constant communication with that neighboring pastor. Otherwise, you may end up programming more of his involvement than he can give.

The specific steps for setting up a council are outlined in *The Practical Guide for Parish Councils* (Twenty-Third Publications, Mystic, CT 06355). You may need to adapt them a bit to fit your situation. But basically, they should work. If they don't, let me know.

Councils for Small Parishes

Q *In a parish of only a hundred families, why do you need a parish council? Why can't the Altar Society or the Men's Club function as a parish council?*

A A parish council is a small scale model of the Christian community called parish. As such it is called, in all its activities, to be a sign of the mission of the church and at the same time to represent the *whole* parish.

Since the Altar Society has only women as members, it doesn't represent the male half of the parish. Besides, the Altar Society generally takes care of the altar and church. It's not responsible for parish administration, education, (CCD, Adult Education) or Christian service.

The Men's Club, with only male members, doesn't represent the parish community either. It may take care of administration, but isn't competent to handle liturgy, CCD and Christian service.

If a parish is very small, its parish council can be drawn to a smaller scale with fewer committees and fewer members. But the size of the council should be determined more by the needs of the parish and the civic community than by the number of families in the parish.

NOTES

1. *Requiem for a Parish* (Westminster, Maryland: Newman Press, 1962), pp. 13-19.
2. "Parish Renewal: A Process, Not a Program" *Origins,* Vol. 8, No. 42, pp. 673-674.
3. "The Complex Task of the Parish," *Origins,* Vol. 8, No. 28, p. 438.
4. Alex Blochlinger, *The Modern Parish Community* (New York: P.J. Kennedy and Sons, 1965), p. 22.
5. Casiano Floristan, *The Parish—Eucharistic Community,* John Byrne, trans. (Notre Dame: Fides Publishers, 1964), p. 19.
6. Floristan, p. 19.
7. Floristan, p. 21.
8. Blochlinger, p. 23.
9. Jean-Paul Audet, *Structures of Christian Priesthood* (New York: Macmillan Co., 1968), p. 97.
10. Blochlinger, p. 44.
11. Blochlinger, p. 43, Note.
12. Blochlinger, p. 75.
13. Blochlinger.
14. Sabbas J. Kilian, OFM, *Theological Models for the Parish* (New York: Alba House, 1977), p. 6.
15. Leonard Swidler, "People, Priests and Bishops in U.S. Catholic History," *Bishops and People* (Philadelphia: The Westminster Press, 1970), pp. 117-118.
16. Swidler, p. 118.
17. Swidler, p. 120.
18. Swidler, p. 122.
19. Kilian, p. 8.
20. Charles Davis, "The Parish and Theology," *The Clergy Review,* Vol. 49 (1964), p. 269.
21. "Constitution on the Sacred Liturgy," *The Documents of Vatican II,* Walter Abbott, Ed., (New York: Guild Press, 1966), Art. 42, p. 152.
22. "Decree on the Bishops' Pastoral Office in the Church," op. cit., Art. 11, p. 403.
23. Charles Davis, "The Parish and Theology," *The Parish in the Modern World,* James D. Crichton, Ed., (London: Sheed and Ward, 1965), p. 122.
24. Blochlinger, pp. 124-125.
25. Kilian, p. 25.

26. Davis, *The Parish in the Modern World,* p. 134.
27. Karl Rahner, "Theology of the Parish," *The Parish from Theology to Practice,* Hugo Rahner, Ed., Robert Kress, Trans., (Westminster, Maryland: Newman Press, 1968), p. 25.
28. Rahner, pp. 28-29.
29. Rahner, p. 30.
30. Rahner, p. 31.
31. Davis, p. 139.
32. Michael Winter, *Blueprint for a Working Church—A Study in New Pastoral Structures* (St. Meinrad, Indiana: Abbey Press, 1973), p. 5.
33. Winter, p. 11.
34. Winter, p. 118.
35. Floristan, pp. 105-106.
36. "Constitution on the Sacred Liturgy," Art. 42, pp. 152-153.
37. "Constitution on the Church," Art. 26, p. 50.
38. "Constitution on the Church," Art. 8, p. 22.
39. *The Ecclesiology of Vatican II,* Matthew J. O'Connell, Trans. (Chicago, Illinois: Franciscan Herald Press, 1974), p. XV.
40. "Pastoral Constitution on the Church in the Modern World," Art. 59, p. 265.
41. "Constitution on the Church," Art. 21, p. 46.
42. "Pastoral Constitution on the Church in the Modern World," Art. 86, p. 300.
43. "Decree on Ecumenism," Art. 4, p. 348.
44. National Conference of Catholic Bishops, *The Parish* (United States Catholic Conference, Washington, D.C., 1980), p. 13.
45. "Catholics and Protestants Today," *Theology Digest,* Fall 1979, p. 258.
46. *Theology Digest,* p. 259.
47. "Statement of the Latin American Bishops, 1979," *Developing Basic Christian Communities* (Chicago, Illinois: National Federation of Priests Councils, 1979), p. 41.
48. *The Shape of the Church to Come* (New York: The Seabury Press, 1974), p. 108.
49. *The Shape of the Church to Come,* pp. 109-110.

BIBLIOGRAPHY

Books

Ad Hoc Committee on the Parish. *Parish Development.* Washington, D.C.: National Conference of Catholic Bishops, 1980.

Adams, Arthur Merrihew. *Effective Leadership for Today's Church.* Philadelphia: The Westminster Press, 1978.

Anderson, James D. *To Come Alive! New Proposal for Revitalizing the Local Church.* New York: Harper & Row, Publishers, 1973.

Audet, Jean-Paul. *Structures of Christian Priesthood.* New York: The Macmillan Co., 1967.

Blochlinger, Alex. *The Modern Parish Community.* Translated by Geoffrey Stevens. New York: P.J. Kennedy & Sons, 1965.

Bravo, Francisco. *The Parish of San Miguelito in Panama.* Cuernavaca, Mexico: Sondeos, 1966.

Clark, Stephen B. *Building Christian Communities: Strategy for Renewing the Church.* Notre Dame: Ave Maria Press, 1972.

Davis, Charles and others. *The Parish in the Modern World.* London: Sheed & Ward, 1965.

Floristan, Casiano. *The Parish—Eucharistic Community.* Translated by John F. Byrne. Notre Dame: Fides Publishers, Inc., 1964.

Foster, John. *Requiem for a Parish.* Westminister, Maryland: The Newman Press, 1962.

Glasse, James D. *Putting It Together in the Parish.* Nashville: Abingdon Press, 1972.

Greeley, Andrew M. *The Church and the Suburbs.* New York: Sheed & Ward, 1959.

Hamer, Jerome, O.P. *The Church Is a Communion.* Translated by Geoffrey Chapman, Ltd., (Ronald Matthews). New York: Sheed & Ward, 1964.

Hinnebusch, Paul, O.P. *Community in the Lord.* Notre Dame: Ave Maria Press, 1975.

Hull, Thomas Patrick, editor. *Developing Basic Christian Communities.* Chicago: National Federation of Priests Councils, 1979.

Kilian, Sabbas J., O.F.M. *Theological Models for the Parish.* New York: Alba House, 1977.

O'Meara, Thomas F. and Donald M. Weisser. *Projections: Shaping an American Theology for the Future.* Garden City, New

York: Doubleday & Co., Inc., 1970.

Rahner, Hugh, S.J., ed. *The Parish from Theology to Practice.* Translated by Robert Kress. Westminster, Maryland: The Newman Press, 1958.

Rahner, Karl, S.J. *The Shape of the Church to Come.* New York: Seabury Press, 1972.

_____ and Daniel Morrissey, O.P., eds. "Theology of Pastoral Action," Vol. 1, *Studies in Pastoral Theology.* New York: Herder & Herder, 1968.

Segundo, Juan Luis, S.J. *The Community Called Church,* Vol. 1. *A Theology for Artisans of a New Humanity.* Trans. John Drury. Maryknoll, New York: Orbis Books, 1973.

Swidler, Leonard and Arlene, ed. and trans. *Bishops and People.* Philadelphia: The Westminster Press, 1969.

Winter, Michael M. *Blueprint for a Working Church: A Study in New Pastoral Structures.* St. Meinrad, Indiana: Abbey Press, 1973.

Articles

Colson, J. "Qu'est-ce qu-un diocese?" *Nouvelle Revue Theologique,* LXXV (1953).

Davis, Charles. "The Parish and Theology," *The Clergy Review,* XLIX (May, 1964), pp. 265-290.

DeWitt, John. "Making a Community out of a Parish," *Cross Currents,* (Spring, 1966), pp. 197-211.

Fitzpatrick, Joseph P. "Parish of the Future," *America,* (Nov. 6, 1965), pp. 521-523.

Grasso, D. "Osservazioni sulla teologia della parrocchia," *Gregorianum,* (1959), pp. 293-314.

Greeley, Andrew M. "The Question of the Parish as a Community," *Worship,* XXXVI, II, pp. 136-143.

Moran, Robert E. "Theology of the Parish," *Worship,* XXXVIII, VII, pp. 156-167.

O'Meara, Thomas. "Karl Rahner on Priest, Parish, and Deacon," *Worship,* 40, pp. 103-110.

Schillebeeckx, E. "The Synod of Bishops: Crisis of Faith and Local Church," *Information and Documentation on the Conciliar Church,* 67-24 (July 23, 1967).

Schurr, Maurice. "The Parish as a Supernatural Reality," *Orate Frates,* 12 (1938), pp. 255-459.

Steeman, T. "Political Relevance of the Christian Community Between Integralism and Critical Commitment," *Concilium,* 84 (1973), pp. 40-47.

INDEX